BE CAREFUL
WITH
GOD'S
DAUGHTER

MARCUS L. BOSTON

UNFAZED PUBLISHING
YOUR MIND IS OUR BUSINESS

TAMPA FLORIDA

Marcus L. Boston

ISBN: 9781959275282

LIBRARY OF CONGRESS : 2023941892

Unless otherwise noted, all Scripture quotations are taken from the King James Version of the Bible.

UNFAZED PUBLISHING

YOUR MIND IS OUR BUSINESS

Marcus L. Boston

Dedication

I dedicate this book to all the daughters of God who desire to be married. I pray this book ministers to you and help you weed out the men of God who say they desire to marry you, but end up breaking your heart. May the Lord help you discern the thoughts and intents of men's hearts that are pursuing you. Be made whole. In Jesus name.

I dedicate this book to all the sons of God who desire to be married who are not playing games. I pray you're built up and rooted in your most holy faith so you can lead confidently in your future marriage. I pray you're healed over the women who hurt you as you searched for your wife. Be made whole. In Jesus name.

Table Of Contents

Preface

As I begin this book, my heart is heavy toward us single people in the Lord. 2023 makes thirty years in the Lord for me. I'm not a novice in the things of God. I've been an armorbearer multiple times, the head of the men's ministry, a praise and worship leader, I was the one trusted to pick up speakers from the airport, I've been in inner circles with pastors as a minister in training, and I've talked with plenty of single women of God throughout these thirty years. I'm the person the saints call when they get caught up. I'm an intercessor and prayer warrior. I love to praise and worship the Lord. I'm straight and love the female anatomy. Women are God's greatest creation to me.

I write this book with the intent of helping us all get on one accord so we can not only complete the work God has given us to do, but also so we single people can get married. Recently I became overwhelmed with phone calls I received from different single women of God pertaining to what single men of God did to them. I jokingly said I was going to write a book about this, but soon thereafter, God gave me this book as an assignment. For those who do not know me, I'm very transparent and this book will be very detailed. You will know exactly what's being said without confusion. May God help us all as we pursue marriage in the name of Jesus.

Chapter One

Are We God's Children?

Men in the church, are you God's sons? I shouldn't have to ask this question, but I have to. If you're a son of God, how are you treating God's daughters? The daughters of God are heirs of the promises of God. They are in the hands of God. They are fearfully and wonderfully made. They are chosen vessels for the Masters use; not yours. To the men in the church who are using the women of God, shame on you. Players shouldn't be in the family of God. If you came to Christ as a player, you will not stay a player in the Lord. Your job is to seek the Lord daily. Study your bible, learn to pray, learn to praise the Lord, and become a worshiper. Your job is to grow in the things of God to reach maturity. Once you reach maturity, if you're still single, you shouldn't be using your maturity in Christ to use God's daughters.

Through the years I've experienced many things being single. Some women call me handsome, they like how I dress, they like my cologne, and now that I'm mature in the things of God, this makes me more attractive than the men sitting on their butts not praising God. I used to be the guy sitting in church looking all hard, not praising God, and looking disinterested. I was fresh out of the world when I came to Christ. I was in my pastor's office every week for months getting rebuked for something I said. The entire story is in my first book, "A Pastor's Mistake. A Transparent Novel Testimony." I didn't know the bible and I had no church character at all. Nonetheless, I grew through the many things I experienced, witnessed, and endured. I studied my bible, I prayed, and I grew in the Lord. I never understood why the daughters of God I desired didn't desire me. I have those answers now. They were mature in the Lord and could clearly see I was ignorant in the things of God. Now that I'm mature in Christ, and several of those women are still single, guess who looks attractive to them now? I start this chapter mainly for the mature sons of God who understand church culture, who clearly perceive, and discern the daughters of God. Daughters of God pay attention to this information.

As a single man of God who's now mature in the faith, I understand that the daughters of God can see me as a potential husband. Depending on their level of attraction to me, will determine if she's interested or not. If I'm exactly what she is looking for, or hoping to have in a husband, this may cause her to seriously desire me and forget about all others. There is a difference between potential husband material, and exactly what she desires in a husband. The potential husbands are men who are kept in her life because they have qualities she desires in a husband. However, there are things missing. One potential husband has certain qualities and another potential has others.

These potential husbands are very different from each other. If only she could combine these potential husbands into one man. She can't make a choice because she desires all of those qualities or characteristics in each man. Honestly, whenever I find out I'm just a potential husband to a certain woman, I exit the situation. If I'm not the clear choice, I make the choice to exit. I used to be that guy who was in competition with other men for a woman's attention and love. I'm not that guy anymore. I don't have the energy or focus to do that again. You can have him or them. Men, how do you know if you're a potential husband? Well, how much time does she have for you? Dating exclusively and dating generally are two different things. If she's the only woman you're dating and you see her once in a while, well, chances are there are other men she's entertaining. I'm just saying. If I'm dating you, I'm serious about you. I don't date multiple ladies at the same time. Men if you're dating other women, then don't worry about it. Y'all are in the same boat. Now if the woman you're dating meets the man she clearly sees as husband, you won't hear from her anymore. It's a wrap.

The man she sees as husband will have her undivided attention. She will forget about those potential husbands in Christ. She will ghost these brothers and don't even know she did it. She will stop returning calls, texts, dms, and emails, once her focus is on the man she sees as her husband. She's about to make room for this man in her life. She's about to seek the Lord about this man. She's about to go on fasts and do everything to get it together. She's about to purge her entire life of those potential husbands. These guys are now history. She is cleaning house. Talk about a woman disappearing. Oh it's happened to me before. A woman of God disappeared and next thing I knew she was married. It happened to me. I dated a new woman of God I saw as wife and stopped talking to the potential wife material. Apparently, she connected with someone at the same time I did. I didn't hear from her anymore and I didn't contact her. When it ended with the woman I saw as wife I was hurt, but I eventually contacted the potential wife material months later. I really took the time to think about the two of us. We had a lot in common and I believed we would be good together as a couple. I now saw her as wife without reconnecting with her. I made up my mind to pursue her. I called her saying I had some news to share and she also had some news to share. She went first and told me she was married. I was like, "Huh? What? For real? I was about to say we should get married." She responded, "No way! You're joking right? Please be joking." "I wasn't joking." I replied feeling like a fool. This is the first time I'm sharing this experience in a book. Yeah, I know. I was very disappointed too. This was the woman of God in "From Woman To Woman Volume Two" who came over to give me some, but changed her mind. When this happened we were both on the road to divorce. We were both in very dark sad places. I missed out on a good woman with her.

Marcus L. Boston

Maybe I'll write a book on the good women I missed out on. By the time my focus went back to her she was married. They decided to marry for the same reasons I called her saying we should get married. Deep huh? Anyway, she saw him as husband and married him. She literally got married the day before I called her. What are the odds? However, my point is made. When a daughter of God sees a man of God as husband, he becomes her focus and all other men are obsolete. It's the same result if both of you are dating multiple people. You both ghosted each other while pursuing other interests at the same time. However, your other interests didn't lead to marriage so now that potential spouse returns to your focal point, but it's too late. You're history.

If I'm a potential husband in a woman's eyes, this puts me in a category within her. There may or may not be other men in this place. It depends on the woman and her place in God. Women who are new Christians are different from women who have twenty years in Christ. There's levels to Christianity. I may not be aware this woman is now paying attention to me and possibly praying to God about me. When you're a man of God who's not playing games, you may not even know this woman is watching you. Why do I say this? If you're in a place with God, your focus is on the things that pertain to God. Although you still have your desire for a wife, God has now become the priority. For you men of God shaking your head, this is the truth. Let me share my backstory and I'll come back to this. I was so full of lust and extremely horny when I first got saved. I was inflamed with sexual passion and tormented by not having sex. I went through a major transformation by God which was not an overnight experience. I love having my mind focused on Jesus. Focused on God keeps my mind at peace. It helps me watch as well as pray. It helps me keep God as my priority. I appreciate not actively looking and searching for a wife presently. I'm sure I will again at some point, but for now, I am seeking first the kingdom of God. When I first came to Christ I had a girlfriend. We were sexually active. I didn't even know what the word fornication meant. Instead of writing this information again, I'll share an excerpt from my book, "A Pastor's Mistake. A Transparent Novel Testimony."

"I gave my life to Christ in August of 1993. At the time the Lord saved me, I had a girlfriend of almost two years. This woman is "Her" in the chapter, "The Whole Package" in my tell-all book, "From Woman To Woman." When I first joined this church, I had never even heard of the word fornication. I remember saying amen when they preached against fornication, not having a clue to what it meant, and that I was the guilty party. I had a thought one day that I should grab my dictionary and look the word up. As I grabbed my dictionary, I had another thought that said, "You don't need to look that word up, you're okay." After hearing the second voice, I put the dictionary down.

A few weeks passed by and I finally grabbed my dictionary, ignoring the thought to put the dictionary back down. I read the entire definition of the word fornication. I screamed out with my whole heart, "NOOOOOOOOO, ANYTHING BUT THAT LORD!!!" I didn't want to give up sex. It was just too good to give up. I loved sex to the fullest; especially with an experienced woman. I didn't want to accept sex outside of marriage as sin. Heck, three weeks was too long for me to go without sex. Now I had to give up sex until I got married; if I ever got married. I really couldn't see how I could abstain and flee fornication. I shook my head in utter disbelief that I could ever abstain from indulging in it." Page 12 paragraph 3. I understand all the struggles of obeying God's word.

Like I was saying, if I'm a potential husband, a woman of God is watching my life. If I'm the only one she's interested in, she may watch me and never shoot her shot as they say these days. I might not be aware of her interest in me. Depending on what I display and how she observes me, will determine if I keep her attention. She could be in my presence and I do something that shatters her interest. You never know who's watching you or who may be interested in you. This is why having good character is important. Not just how you represent Christ, but how you present and represent yourself. If I'm exactly what she desires, she could have us introduced or she may ask me out. In my opinion, Ruth laying at Boaz feet was her shooting her shot. It's amazing how many women have shared how they liked me, but I never approached them. I told them I never knew you were interested. By the time they told me they were dating someone. Why tell me you were interested if you've moved on? If I never knew why tell me now? This doesn't make any sense to me. Please don't think all men are paying attention to you. If God is first in his life pray this prayer, "Lord, I'm interested in brother "such in such," if this is your will, let him see me Lord. Reveal me to him if this be your will. In Jesus name. Amen." This is a good way to help get noticed. I appreciate, "Just Whiti." She has so many jokes about shooting her shot on social media. She's a very funny woman of God. Check her out. Now if God answers this prayer, if this happens and you two begin dating/courting, do not have sex under no circumstances. Why am I saying this? Well, you're about to find out why now.

The book of Genesis chapter 3 verse 16 says, "and thy desire shall be to thy husband, and he shall rule over thee." I pondered on this verse. This is a portion of the woman's punishment for eating the fruit from the tree of the knowledge of good and evil. Why is it a punishment to desire your husband? Shouldn't she desire her husband? This is very interesting to me. The Amplified bible says, "Yet your desire and craving will be for your husband, and he will rule over you." The Amplified verse goes deeper into the meaning. Let's look at the definitions of these words.

Craving – A consuming desire; a yearning.

Yearning – An intense or overpowering longing, desire, or need; craving.

Desire – To wish or long for; want.
   To want to have sex with.
   To express a wish for; request.

I've never heard anyone ever preach or teach on this portion of the scripture. Everyone focuses on child bearing or men being the head of the woman. I've never heard anyone declare what I'm about to share. I'm sure your mind is already thinking. I decided to look desire up on www.blueletterbible.org to see if it's the same interpretation. Desire is the word "teshuqah." H8669 (Tesh-oo-kaw) means desire, longing, and craving. It's the same meaning. I believe this is why many women of God strongly desire to be married. I believe this is why so many women of God are excited about being a wife. God already told Adam it wasn't good for him to be alone. Now God says to the woman that her desire shall be to her husband. Women desire sex with their future husband. I've heard many of these jokes. "Wait until I get married. I'm gonna put it on my husband." I've heard plenty of these. I have my own joke in my book, "A Pastor's Mistake." - I said, *"I can't wait for God to give me my wife. I can't wait to have my rib. When God gives me my rib, I'm going to put some barbeque sauce on it."* The whole church exploded into laughter and I didn't know it at the time, but I created a *slogan in our church. Many singles had their own barbeque sauce jokes".*- Paragraph 1 page 47.

Singles who abstain imagine their wedding day and wedding night. Daughters imagine it more. Daughters fantasize about it. They are thinking of their wedding dress, the venue, maid of honor, bridesmaids, and most of all, their wedding night. This is a very big dream. How she hopes to be touched, kissed, fondled, and caressed. Her lingerie, the suite, and music are perfect. Her hair, nails, toes, and makeup must be flawless. She wonders what her husband will wear for her on this special first night of becoming one as husband and wife. She looks forward to indulging with all liberty and sexual freedom. This sexual experience will not be sin. Unless you're "a real virgin," every sexual experience prior to tonight was sin. No matter how good that sex was prior to marriage, it was sin and God was not pleased. There will be no repentance tonight. No shame. No guilty tears. No condemnation. This is the promised land for all singles in the Lord. No more lonely nights. No more tears because your body is hot and horny. To yield to those fiery passions was sin. But tonight and every day or night after this, it's not sin. Now all of her secret places will be explored, discovered, revealed, and God approves. Her husband has obtained favor with God because he found her. She imagines how she desires to please her husband. She's been waiting on this night to manifest. The two, now one, have entered into the pages of the book of Song Of Solomon. Best believe these wedding night thoughts are intense and passionate. Most daughters of God desire to have their husband just how it's declared in Genesis. They crave and want him now. Not later. He's long overdue in the eyes of many daughters. How many sons of God are thinking about their wedding night? Probably not many. Honestly, maybe the sons who are abstaining from sex and believing God to find his wife.

So daughters of God, there is nothing wrong with desiring your future husband. Just watch as well as pray as it pertains to the sons of God. When you meet a man of God that you can clearly see as your husband, you need to seek the Lord. Chances are this man will turn you on sexually by just looking at him. The more you learn about him the more you're possibly turned on. If you find yourself in this place one day, under no circumstances do you have sex with him before marriage. Make no provision for the flesh to fulfill the lusts thereof. Roman chapter 13 v. 14. You don't need to be at his residence, at all, and he doesn't need to be at your residence, ever. If you believe this man is your husband, make him wait until your wedding night. Be faithful to Jesus. No sex of any kind. Don't do anything that could bring an orgasm. I know exactly what I just said. Don't set yourself up for failure. Be sober thinking. You don't know this man. Let's say you do know this man, still be sober minded. Don't let your flesh cause your mind to become completely carnal towards this man.

Deep passionate kisses can lead to sex. Ask God for temperance. It's a fruit of the Holy Ghost / Spirit. If you're entirely weak towards this man, and you know for a fact that your body is "his" without marriage, never be alone with him; period. Pray and have those you trust praying with you. Keep the Lord first daughters. Don't yield. He shouldn't be making any sexual advances anyway, and neither should you. Don't lose sight or focus on the Lord. Men of God don't tempt her. If she is your gift from God, respect and honor her. Honor God by honoring her. Are you both bought with a price? Are you a son and daughter of God? Keep the word of God. No excuses. "God know I'm human and have needs." Yeah ok. How did you get those needs? Where did these needs come from? Sin? Fornication? Your so called needs came from sin. What about your righteous needs? I wrote a book for us entitled, "I'm Burning! Abstinence Tools For Single Christians." This book is for those of us who's flesh stays horny because we have a big sexual appetite we developed in sin. This book is very detailed sexually. Ladies once you've given him your body there's nothing else to give. Your body is the prize. Your body is the trophy. Your body is the gem. Your body is priceless. Once you've given him your body there's no need to marry you. I've seen plenty of women of God walk around looking ashamed once she's exposed for having sex with a brother in church. Most times they backslide or leave the church for a season because of the embarrassment. Why are you embarrassed? Why are you ashamed? Lots of men walk around with that accomplished look knowing they had you sexually. I'm guilty of this. I'll share what I did and how it happened later on in this book. Please daughters don't give up your body before marriage. Change how you see your body for those of you who are very sexually experienced, and who are new Christians fresh from the world. "I have sexual needs." You should have righteous needs. You need to seek God. You need to pray and abstain. You need healing and deliverance. You need wholeness from past relationships and sexual encounters. These should become your needs. A daughter of God's body is so valuable that in the Old Testament all daughters had to be virgins. No man desired a woman who wasn't a virgin. Deuteronomy chapter 22 v. 13-21. On the wedding night the new wife had sex with her new husband on her back. A sheet was laid under her to catch the blood from her hymen being broken. The blood on the sheet was called, "The Tokens Of Virginity." It was proof and evidence she was a virgin. If there was no blood she wasn't a virgin. The daughter was stoned to death in the presence of her father because she wasn't a virgin. Verse 21 is the kicker. "To play the whore in her father's house." Wow! Because she wasn't a virgin she was called a whore. Whore covers a lot of different negative activities. Well, thank God for the grace of God through Jesus. It would be nice if virginity was positively popular and valuable by the masses today.

This is mind blowing to me. So this man married her, had sex with her, she wasn't a virgin which made him angry, and now she's stoned to death. He still had sex with her. Now he's free to marry again. He's free to move on to the next woman. I wonder how many times did this cycle repeat itself? The daughters who knew they weren't virgins, I wonder what were their thoughts going into the marriage? Were they hoping he loved them, or their body, so much that he didn't care? Oh, most people weren't in love before they got married back then. No dating. No courtship. Sometimes strangers got married. Their father gave them away to the man who could pay the right price for his virgin. Are you starting to see why the man was so angry now? He paid for a virgin. This was not about love. The daughter had no say so. I wonder if the father had to give back everything he received for his daughter since she wasn't a virgin. How embarrassing for the father. There was no redemption for his daughter. She was stoned to death and he witnessed it.

Like I was saying, your body is valuable daughters. Once you've given up your body there is nothing left to give. In the cases for those Old Testament daughters, they had sex with at least one man that didn't marry them. Whore covers a lot of ground, but I want to think of a scenario that I believe took place some of the time. I wonder how many of them were told, "You know I love you and want to marry you. I just don't have enough resources right now to pay your father what he's asking for you.

Please don't make me wait. Let's make love now. You know I'm going to marry you." I'm sure most of these daughters didn't just give their virginity to a nobody. Fornication cost them their life. Being stoned to death was brutal. I'm sure some of those daughters were molested or raped, and just like many women are today they didn't inform anyone. I'm sure some of those daughters just wanted to get married one day and have a wedding night knowing they would be stoned to death the following day. Virgin women were sought after. If you weren't a virgin you were last to be chosen. You weren't as valuable as the virgins. Your body is valuable women of God.

Those men expected to get the virgin they paid for and that's why they were so angry. A good example of a man angry that someone had sex with his woman is the movie, "The Best Man." Lance was engaged to Mia. She was a virgin when they were first introduced to each other in college by Harper Lance's friend. He was so proud because he was the first and the only one she ever had sex with. He was so happy no one else had her sexually. Lance valued this about Mia. However, Lance cheated on her many times and Mia wanted sweet revenge. She made sexual advances toward Harper and Harper yielded to Mia. They shared one night of pleasure. Lance was furious when he found out he wasn't the only one who had sex with Mia. He beat the crap out of Harper who was now his best man, and called off the wedding. Isn't this something? A whorish man who had plenty of women sexually, and cheated on his woman many times, was angry his woman gave her body to another man. She cheated on Lance and this broke him down. I suppose the anger Lance displayed was probably the same anger those Old Testament husbands had discovering their wives weren't virgins. The female anatomy is priceless.

Daughters I know it's not easy when you're in the presence of the man you see as your future husband. If you haven't experience this yet, well, you will. Your body is for marriage and you're not presently married. So, if you give him your body, what's your excuse? What is the reason? Is it love? Is this pleasing God? It's definitely not love and God is not pleased. If he loved you he would honor God by waiting until you were married. If you love him don't tempt him. Please don't give your body to him. There are many men of God who play the game very well, but have no intention on marrying you. Here's a good word of advice: if he doesn't clearly see you as his wife you need to leave him alone. Make sure you're not just potential wife material to him. This man needs to make it known you're the only one he desires and there is no one else. Now if you're dating other men, well, never mind. If you see him as husband make sure he sees you as wife. If you're potential wife material, then you might be one of many he's dating. If you see him as husband, you need to ask him the truth and find out if you're the only one he's dating. If he says you're the only one he's pursuing, (after God only) you should be his priority. Make sure his character is real. Do not be impressed if he can pray, prophesy, and speak in tongues. He's supposed to be able to do those things. Do not be impressed if he can sing and preach. Do not be impressed if he's one of these "high powered men" as they call them these days. Don't be impressed if he has great status. Don't be impressed with his house, his cars, or financial success. Don't be impressed with the anointing in his life. The gifts and calls are without repentance. Just because he's better looking or doing better than most men of God doesn't make him a good catch. Do not be in competition with other women of God over him. Don't chase after a man who isn't running to you. If he's running from you stop chasing him. This is a big NO! Don't do it. If you're not the clear choice exit. This is what I do when I find out the woman I'm dating is dating other men. I exit. If I'm not the clear choice it's time to move on. Do not try to sex a man into marriage. It's not going to work. In the end you'll regret it. Be sober minded. Make sure you're not lusting for a man "like him." Be clear thinking. Most of all, ask God this very specific prayer: "God is (his name) abstaining from sex? Is he a man of integrity and honorable? Will he be a faithful husband? Is he a player? Is he dating multiple women? Lord reveal his heart and intention towards me. In Jesus name. Amen." Prayer this kind of prayer in your own way. God is faithful. He will reveal the truth. The truth can be painful. If God reveals he's a dog don't be in denial. Believe God. Don't say, "Imma see for myself." like Ariel Fitz says in her jokes on social media. Ladies if you're abstaining and waiting on your husband from God, do you want a man who is continuously having sex every chance he gets? Here's what I told a brother in Christ who was bragging that he had five women he's sleeping with. I suppose he thought I was going to be impressed. I rebuked him. I guess the other men of God didn't rebuke him because he looked stunned by my words. Here's what I said after I rebuked him in the name of Jesus, "So, you got five women? (He said yes.) And you're sexing all five of them? (Yes.) Do you want a wife? (Yes) So, why should God give you one of His daughters? (Because I'm a good man.) What makes you a good man? You just said you're sleeping with five different women. (I know how to treat a woman. I will please her and make her happy. I'll take care of her. I'll be faithful.) Interesting. I'm not going to say God is not going to give you a wife since you're sexing five different women. God is faithful. (He's nodding thinking I'm about to say something good.) Well, God will give you a woman who's doing exactly what you're doing. (His face contorted. He's looking disgusted and repulsed.) See that feeling you're having right now, that's how you feel about yourself. (He got mad.) That disgusted look is how you feel about yourself. (No it's not.) Yes it is. Ok then, why is the thought of marrying a woman having sex with five different men nasty to you? (He didn't answer.) That's what you're doing. You would say she's a hoe right? (Right.) You're the hoe. You don't have five women. Five women have you. I'm not trying to make you mad, but you're a hoe. God is not about to give you His best and you're not His best for her." This brother is in position at a church. He's called on by his pastor to do things and to handle church business. This son of God wants a woman who's a holy angel and he's living like a lust demon. How many men of God feel exactly like this brother? Be honest with yourself. You say you want to be a husband, but you're a hoe. Not to mention you're going to reap these deeds you're doing. In the world players are respected, but you're not respected by God. The biblical term for player is whoremonger. What daughter of God wants a whore for a husband? No abstinence equals no self-control. You have no self-restraint. You're required by God to present your body as a living sacrifice, holy, and acceptable unto God which is your reasonable service. Romans chapter 12 v. 1. Men of God it's time to really live right. This is your warning. Women of God, daughters of God, stop giving up your body. I heard several ordained ministers talking about a woman inside the church. They talked about who hit it, what she does sexually, and even brought up the fact she didn't have on any panties that day. I shook my head in disbelief. I was standing nearby and heard them talking. Men of God are telling everything y'all did sexually to other men of God, and they continue to spread it. Sounds like gossip fellas. Men who desire to be married, who are interested in you might be turned off hearing about you with their brother in Christ. Listen fellas, all whoremongers shall have their part in the lake of fire and brimstone. Revelation chapter 21 v. 8. Repent and allow God to change your ways before he judges you. You may die instantly and what will be your reward if you die as a player? Hell. Enough is enough. It's sad that many of these single men of God are on platforms preaching, praying, prophesying, and having sex with as many women as possible in the church. Many hold positions in leadership. Men of God your body is for marriage. Your body is for your wife from God. Men there are women of God who don't want a man who's been a player / whoremonger. Why are you guys bragging to other guys about the women you had sex with in the church? You're pointing them out and arrogant about it. This reminds me of the woman caught in adultery. She was brought before Jesus, but where was the man she was having sex with? Why wasn't he brought before Jesus as well? Deuteronomy chapter 22 v. 22. This verse says they both shall die, but they only brought the woman. It was probably one of the men in their circle and this is why they were caught; excuse me, she was caught. These men pointed her out to be possibly stoned to death while the man was free to live. Isn't this something? Doesn't this relate to today? The men point out the woman of God who had sex with a man of God, she is judged, but the man of God isn't judged correctly. I added correctly because a judgment by the word of God has no respect of persons. Men who are still respected after having sex with a daughter of God will reap what they sowed by the hand of God. Men are you a son of God or not? Or are you of your father the devil? Do you really believe you can use a woman of God and there be no consequences? Do you know the Lord? Do you think the grace of God is sufficient to continue being a whoremonger? You're in positions in your church. You're on flyers, you're in ministry, you're singing, you're playing instruments, you're prophesying, you're teaching, and you know the bible very well, yet your life doesn't reflect the bible. You know what you're doing is wrong, but you continue in it like God doesn't see you. You act like you have exemption from God's judgement. Then you have the nerve to brag about having sex with these women. You know these women see you as husband and you play the game until you get what you want. You're just like the sons of Eli. God judged them.

"Wherefore the sin of the young men was very great before the Lord: for men abhorred the offering of the Lord." First Samuel chapter 2 v. 17. The sons of Eli were priests. They held position in the work of the Lord, and they hated the offering of the Lord. Very sad these men of God who were in position had evil hearts. Let's continue. "Now Eli was very old, and heard all that his sons did unto all Israel; and how they lay with the women that assembled at the door of the tabernacle of the congregation." v.22 While you men are talking about the women you had sex with you're getting a reputation yourself. "And he said unto them, Why do ye such things? For I hear of your evil dealings by all this people." v.23. You're not even struggling to live right. You have chosen to live wrong entirely. The grace of God is for the struggles while you're being converted, while you're being delivered, and while you're being changed by the word of God. You're not trying to change. You're not honoring God at all while you're doing His work. Eli addressed the sins of his sons, but he honored his sons above the Lord. v.29. Read chapter 2 until the end of chapter 4. Eli judged Israel forty years. Chapter 4 v. 18. Eli was the authority. He should have kept God first, but he didn't. He let his sons have sex with women of the congregation of Israel, and notice, the sons of Eli didn't marry any of them. They got plenty of sex and didn't get married. They used the daughters of God. After what I shared earlier, do you see how serious this is? If these women were virgins, if they were chosen for marriage, they will be stoned to death. If these women were married, they were in adultery and should be put to death along with the sons of Eli. This was a big mess! The word of God was being transgressed greatly and Eli did nothing. Why? He would have to judge his sons by the word of God. Well, Eli didn't judge his sons so God came and judged Eli and his sons. All of you pastors who know the men in your church are whoremongers, you know the men in your congregations are sleeping with many women in your church, and you have them in positions, God is going to deal with you. You better rebuke and correct them while you can. God's judgment will come at some point. These women who were used by these whoremongers are crying out to God in pain and horror because they were victims of game in the house of God. So many daughters were made to think they were the only woman. They were told they were exactly what he was asking God to bring him, but it wasn't true. Then you got the nerve to spread how and what sexual activities you had with her to the men in your church. You're such a proud hoe. God sees you. How do you feel knowing you've hurt so many daughters of God? No remorse. You don't even care do you? You will care soon enough. God is going to deal with you. It's time to change. It's time to repent and really seek God with your whole heart. Turn away from your wicked ways before God judges you. "Who are you to judge me Marcus?" Well, God told me to write this book. I'm not judging you. I'm obeying God. God desires you to yield all of yourself to Him so He doesn't have to judge you. You're still going to reap what you sowed whether you repent or not, but it would be better if you repent and allow God to change you.

Have I ever used a daughter of God sexually? Well, all of my sexual experiences are in my tell-all, "From Woman To Woman" book series. Reader discretion is advised. 18+ readers only. In my thirty years in Christ, I've had three women accuse me of using them. All three situations are in my books. Did I use them?

Woman number 1 is called "Church Girl" in my tell-all book series. She was anointed and popular in the church scene. I told this woman of God that I wasn't interested in her. She didn't take what I said seriously. I couldn't believe what happened. I told her I wasn't interested, but she insisted on trying to change my mind. I was abstinent almost three years when she and I had sex. Here's what I wrote in my book, "From Woman To Woman Volume Two."

The very next day after church, our pastor asked me to give Church Girl a ride home. I sincerely didn't want to do it because the Chicago Bulls were on television that day. I agreed to give her a ride and as I was dropping her off, she invited me inside. I didn't want to go in. I wanted to get home to watch the game. She said she had some greens, rice, fried chicken, cornbread, and string beans already prepared. On that note, I went inside. It was better than the hotdogs and fries I was going to eat.

After I received my big plate of food, I watched the Bulls in peace. I don't know where she went, but she let me watch the game alone. I don't know exactly how long she was gone, but I did notice her when she returned. She was standing about ten feet to my left as I watched the Chicago Bulls. When a commercial came on, I looked over at Church Girl. I couldn't believe my eyes. This woman took off those regular church clothes she had on, and had on a minidress that was fitted at her midthigh. I didn't know she even had attire like this. As soon as my eyes were fixed on her, she bent over with her hands flat on the wall. There was nothing shy at all about this. These words exited my mouth immediately, "UH, BRING ALL OF THAT OVER HERE!" She smiled and walked toward me with that I want you look I grew to love with previous women. I forgot the game was even on. I put that plate aside as Church Girl walked towards me. Once she was standing in front of me, I pulled the skirt up and got a real good look at her from the waist down. I turned her around with the skirt up so I could see those curves from every angle. I couldn't believe all of this sexiness was under those old women clothes. (We had sex. Here's what happened immediately afterwards.)

"All of a sudden, I began to cry very hard and couldn't stop crying. I wept very bitterly as we were on her couch naked. I had many issues, but I wanted to please God. Church Girl didn't cry as I did. When I looked over at her, she had her hand on her head, and appeared sad to me. After I stopped crying, I said to her, "I'm so sorry. I had no intention on this happening with us. Please forgive me." I said out loud in front of her, "God, I'm sorry for sinning. I repent. Please forgive me." Church Girl didn't say anything. I got dressed and didn't bother to freshen up before I left. I wanted to take a shower in my own bathroom."

I had no intentions on losing my testimony. At this time in my personal walk, this was a big achievement for me. Not only was this devastating for me, but this opened the door to me being backslidden. We were both members of the same church and when two people had sex before marriage, they always ran to the courthouse to get married. I didn't. She even asked me why haven't I married her. I repeated those same words I told her from the beginning, "I'm not interested in you." Sex will never get me to marry you. She grew up in the church. I didn't. I was fresh out of the world with no church foundation. I still looked like the world and she always wanted a man like me; well, that's what she told me. I can't speak for other men. I've seen many men run to the courthouse after they had sex with a daughter of God. They wanted to make it right. Well, you can't make sin right. How do you make sin right? Ask God for forgiveness and repent. I believe the saints run to the courthouse to make it right is based on a scripture. I'll share this shortly. Did I use her? No I didn't. This anointed woman of God seduced me. She saw me as her husband and gave me her body trying to get me to marry her. Even though I told her I wasn't interested in her, she didn't care. She craved me. Neither one of us had any restraint at all. Having sex with her messed up my mind and I couldn't pray, read my bible, or praise and worship God anymore. I went almost three years without sex. Three weeks was too long for me to go without sex in the world. It was a real fight to abstain because I love sex. Between a woman's legs is paradise. I was 25 and had my own apartment. I worked at the United States Postal Service. I had a 1988 Oldsmobile Cutlas which was paid off, and I stayed horny. No children. I was doing pretty well. I was a young Christian and didn't understand the depths of this experience with Church Girl. I didn't lead her on. I didn't play games. I didn't play her. She played herself. I said all of that to say this. Daughters of God, if any man declares he's not interested in you, please leave him alone. There's nothing else to say or do. Do not pray for him to like you. Praying for him to like you when he's already informed you he's not interested is witchcraft. You're praying against his will. God doesn't go against our will. Please leave him alone. Your body is not going to change him. Let me be more detailed: your sexual skills is not going to make him marry you. Here's the verse I said I would share, "If a man find a damsel that is a virgin, which is not betrothed, and lay hold on her, and lie with her, and they be found; Then the man that lay with her shall give unto the damsel's father fifty shekels of silver, and she shall be his wife; because he hath humbled her, he may not put her away all of his days." Deuteronomy chapter 22 v. 28-29. This verse is special to me because it's connected to woman number 2 who I will talk about next. I believe this verse ties with why people run to the courthouse after fornicating to make it right. This verse details a man caught in premarital sex with a virgin woman who wasn't engaged to be married. He was forced to marry her and he had to pay the father in silver. This man couldn't divorce her no matter what happened in their marriage. Very interesting huh? Yep. So, do you believe I used woman number 1?

Woman number 2. This one can be very debatable. We had an argument over what happened between us. She said I used her and I declared I didn't use her. We were friends, but became the best of strangers for a season. Here's what I wrote in my book, "I'm Burning. Abstinence Tools For Single Christians" page 84 – 86. *We were friends and yes, we both were attracted to each other. We are now strangers and do not talk anymore. Here's why. One day we were alone and wrestling. This was something we did on a regular basis. However, on this day she ended up on top of me in a straddling position. When I looked up seeing her straddling me, a fleshly trigger exploded inside of me. I looked away from her and began to say quickly, "I quit. I quit. I quit. Please get off of me!" She was still in play mode. I repeated myself and she was still in play mode speaking, "No! You got beat up by a girl! How do you feel now?" Then I got quiet and slowly said, "Can you please... get off... of me?" I was trying to think of something else, but it seemed impossible to focus on anything else with her fine self straddling me. Then I looked up at her again while she was straddling me. That fleshly trigger had me turned on and I continued to get more turned on as she was on top of me. She was still in play mode. One last time, but in a very relaxed and horny manner I whispered, "Please, get off me." She replied in a non-playful manner, "No, I'm not getting off of you." We just looked at each other and her facial expression changed right before my eyes when she realized she was straddling my fully erected penis. One final time, I asked her to move and she refused. I leaned up quickly, pulled her t-shirt up, and began sucking her breasts. She held me close and didn't try to stop me. We began kissing, rubbing, and touching until our clothes started coming off. As I began sliding her panties down, I heard the Lord say, "Do you really want to humble your sister?!" I jumped back from her and I said, "I gotta go!" I put my clothes on and left. I knew that was God and I also knew that was a scripture in the bible. She and I never discussed what happened that afternoon and when we talked on the phone, it was as if it never happened. She and I were as we were before so it seemed, but it happened again in a different way. This time she complained of her feet hurting so I massaged her feet. This was also normal for us. I actually massaged her feet quite often. However, this time she was already in sex mode and I was just in a normal mode. I was just running my mouth talking to her while she wasn't saying anything. She began to move her feet and legs in a very slow manner which caught my attention. If you read, "A Pastor's Mistake," you already know how I enjoy that I want you look women give. I turned to look at her, and she had that I want you look just gazing at me, and Lord knows she is fine. Looking at her triggered my flesh and we went at it again. The Holy Spirit spoke to me this time as well, and I stopped us again. Even though these two encounters took place, I was actually in a* place of prayer and the Lord was able to intervene. I also asked the Lord to keep me from fornication and I gave Him permission to speak to me when I'm in the process of doing wrong.

Then I had some situations occur in my life that had me stressed out. My focus was all off and I stopped praying. I began to worry about it and I lost my joy. Not long after I entered into this place, I began complaining about everything going wrong. I found myself daydreaming of sex and masturbating. One day my phone rang and although I wanted to stay home, I ended up going out to dinner with her. We went out to eat and afterwards she was inviting me into her place to chill for a moment. I already knew where I was and didn't even want to go in. She kept asking and I kept saying I need to go home. We went back and forth for several minutes. I finally agreed to stay a bit. Here's my actually thought in full transparency, "Lord, if we get caught up tonight, please don't speak to me. If we get caught up tonight, I'm going to hit this." Yes, I really thought those words; sad I know. When she came back into the living room, I immediately noticed those little shorts she changed into. I strongly thought while looking at those little shorts, "Yeah, I'm gonna hit this tonight." After sitting on the couch watching television for some time, we began kissing and went from there. I ended up spending the night and no the Lord didn't say anything to me. We continued fornicating for several months until her period was late. It came a few weeks later after we did *a bunch of repenting and praying. We eventually started talking about getting married and discovered we had some areas of difference that we couldn't compromise. I wish this never took place and the friendship we once had is forever gone.*

Did I use this daughter of God? What do you think? Like I said it's debatable. In my mind I didn't use her, but I understood her point of view. In her mind I acted as if I didn't want it, but I was setting her up for later. Daughters of God, one thing I've learned before Christ and also while fighting to abstain, when I say "no" to women it's like I said yes. Something about saying no made women sexually aggressive to change my mind. Daughters of God, if a man telling you no turns you on, bring it to God in prayer. This information is in this book so you ladies can add this to your prayer life. Here's the truth: if God didn't speak to me the first time we would have had sex then. You just read that verse a little earlier. Humble has many definitions, and I was shocked by it also meaning to lower in value. Can women be seen as unvaluable? Well, let's talk about that for a moment. I know several women who have reputations for having sex with lots of men. What is the popular saying? "You can't turn a whore into a housewife." Well, Jesus can. God is saving porn stars, prostitutes, and strippers. If God saves you, God has a plan for you, and ladies, God has a husband for you regardless of your past. Same thing for men. Thank God for His grace.

Woman number 3. She said I used her. I said I didn't use her, but her point of view is credible against me. She's in my book, "From Woman To Woman Volume Three." She's in the chapter named, "Remarkable." Now this woman and I were dating. I wasn't dating the first two women I talked about. This was very serious and we were pursuing marriage. Here's what happened.

One day when I had the day off from work, I had an idea that I should surprise her. I gave myself a fresh haircut, took a good shower, and wore something I knew she loved on me. I even wore her favorite cologne she appreciated on me. When she exited public transit, she was so surprised to see me waiting for her. We hugged, she complimented me, I got her door, and we headed on our way. We went to one of her favorite places for food and decided to eat the meal at her house. The children were watching television and we went in her bedroom to eat. While we ate our food, we were listening to a Facebook Live preaching message. It was a good message too. The children came into the bedroom while we listened and wanted some of our food. We didn't want to share any lol. This was so funny and Remarkable put them out so we could hear the message without distraction.

By the time this message ended, it was late and I was feeling sleepy. I was preparing to leave when she asked me stay a little longer. I stayed without a second thought. We were talking about different things and next thing I know, we started kissing. These were the type of kisses that sent surges through my body as our lips and tongue engaged. I was laying on my back. She was on my left side, over me as we kissed. Perfect chemistry every time. We kissed and rubbed on each other. This was the first time I gripped her as we kissed. She had on a crop top and legging shorts. Her body was so soft and this time when we kissed, I was entirely moving in the flow of our energy. My blood was flowing and when her hand grabbed it, I reacted, "Wait! I got to go! I don't have strength!" I sat up quickly as I said those words. Remarkable practically shouted, "NO! DON'T GO!... I GOT STRENGTH!" as she put her hands on my shoulders refraining me from leaving her bed. We both looked at each other in the moment and I finally released, "Ok. I'll stay since you got strength." I laid back down with her hands still on my shoulders.

We went back to kissing and rubbing. I was completely submerged in our sexual energy at this point and Remarkable's touch made me even more horny for her. (edited)

We had sex and I spent the night. We talked about waiting and we did for several months with no issues. After we had sex everything changed immediately with us. I was far from a babe when this happened. The enemy now had access because we broke our hedge of protection. I biblically knew more than her and tried to teach her many things. Here's what happened.

I couldn't believe we became a dating experience of confusion and misunderstandings. The fun died. The good times ended. Our dates became boring. Our great conversations no longer existed and now I had to repeat everything we talked about during our previous conversation. After a month of this, I was tormented by our dating experience. Nothing happening with us made any sense and I couldn't put my finger on the confusion. I was clueless. Nowadays I understand what happened, but when this occurred then, I didn't have any idea of what was taking place. As everything concerning us died, I no longer wanted it. I now despised that we had sex. I began thinking this is the reason why it all fell apart. We broke the hedge of protection and now this is the result. I didn't know what to do and no matter how I tried to talk about our situation, she didn't remember anything the next day. I truly mean this and I started thinking she had a mental issue. Again, I didn't know what to do or how to pray about this. I couldn't imagine living like this for the rest of my life and I believed it was best to end this dating experience. We had a long talk when I broke it off with Remarkable. By the time this conversation was over, there would be no friendship with us. There was some bitterness, or something, on her part towards me. In her eyes, I just wanted to hit it and quit it. In her mind, I hid behind the bible to get between her legs. After we had sex I avoided being alone with her. I was trying to avoid further sexual sin. I also did this with Baby Love (Another character in my book.) and she took this the wrong way as well. I'm trying to live holy! These Christian women I date aren't trying to avoid having sex! So Remarkable is calling me a hypocrite, and proclaiming I used her. I invested a lot just for one night of sex, and I almost died with her. I would never use the bible to get sex. If I was running game, I wouldn't talk about Jesus ever! Let's kick it and give that booty up asap As quickly as possible! I know God is real and I wouldn't dare use His name to get some or receive oral sex. This pissed me off! (edited)

So, in your opinion, did I use her? Her point of view has a good argument. After we had sex I avoided us being alone, but we still dated exclusively. From her point of view, I hit it, I changed, and broke up with her. Well, this is true in the general sense. She completely left out my side of course. Isn't this what we do most times? We don't share the other persons point of view. You should never completely accept one side as the complete truth. Just take it as information until you require more facts. You should ask, "Well, what did you do to them?" Even the word of God says, "He that is first in his own cause seemeth just; but his neighbor cometh and searcheth him." Proverbs chapter 18 v. 17. How many people search out the other side? Not many when it comes to gossip, slander, and backbiting. So many women agreed with her. Oh, she told those around us that we had sex. I am a man of God and this brought me great reproach. My name became mud. I was talked about very badly. Once our entire church knew we had sex, the entire atmosphere of our church was negative against me. As soon as I entered the sanctuary, I received a very bad headache every service and I had this headache during the entire time I was in the sanctuary. When

I left the sanctuary the headache left me immediately. I was no longer free to praise and worship the Lord in my church. People in leadership stopped talking to me altogether. They walked passed me without speaking and talked to the person a few feet from me. I'm not exaggerating. This situation was so bad I resigned from my church simultaneously giving up the position I held in leadership. I didn't defend myself. Once the hearts of a church are against you, especially in the leadership, it's over. I moved on because I had to. There was no more grace to be at this church. I wasn't removed from my position by our pastor, maybe I beat him to it, but I was no longer respected. If I left Remarkable when I had the strength, this would have never happened. I hated this situation. I was accused of hitting it and quitting it. What did I learn in this situation? I learned that the grace I once had years ago no longer existed. My grace was when I had the strength to leave. I should have left with the grace. I trusted her. She said she had strength and I took her at her word. She knew I wanted to wait until marriage. Maybe she lied so we could have sex. Maybe she got exactly what she really wanted out of me, but wasn't thinking things would change. Only God knows. However, what I do know is this: there's always consequences to sin. You can ask for forgiveness. You can repent. However, no matter what, we really do reap what we sow. I reaped confusion and reproach. I reaped being tormented during our church services. Was it worth it? Not at all.

Where I am presently in the Lord I cannot afford anymore setbacks. I'm not dating at moment, and because I posted this on social media, a prophetess asked me if I was lgbtq. I answered with one word; nope. Why ask me this question? Seeking the Lord and being in a good place in God should be viewed as a good thing. I desire to be married and I'm believing God to find the real wife for me in His timing. I desire to be a very good husband. Like I was saying, I no longer have the grace I had as a babe, or young Christian, to have premarital sex. I'm anointed in multiple ways and the enemy would love to trap me, bind me, and get me caught up in sin to discredit me. I'm doing all I can to stay free. God requires more from me now. God desires us all to grow in grace and come to a mature place in Him where we love living for God without sexual reservations for our flesh. Too many of us have sexual reservations in our hearts. We want to try it out before we get married. The only issue is if the sex is bad. What if there is bad sexual chemistry? Now you move on because you couldn't imagine being married with bad sex. Where is God in this? This is not biblical. Remarkable was a good daughter of God I missed out on because I sinned with her. We were good until sexual sin entered. God gave me the strength to leave and I didn't. I reaped what I sowed. You're going to reap what you sow. At some point grace runs out once you're in maturity and know better. You cannot continue in sin and think grace is going to cover your sins. God is faithful and just to forgive us, but we cannot continue in sin hoping God doesn't expose us. We had sex one time after dating for months and it cost me greatly. I believe if all of us singles in the Lord would all seek God with all of our hearts, there would be so many more marriages. Put the games aside, seek the Lord, honor God's word, flee all sexual sins, fall in love with God, worship Him, allow God to lead you and guide you into all truth. This truth will lead us all to our spouse. Men let's all respect and honor all of the daughters of God. Women of God please respect and honor all men of God. Let's not tempt or use each other sexually.

Have I ever been used sexually? Yes. On one occasion, a woman of God told me the truth after we had sex. The character Judy in my book, "A Pastor's Mistake" on page 371 said there's two other guys she wants to have sex with before she settles down. She let me know immediately what happened with us wasn't going to lead to dating or a relationship. This is the one time as a Christian that I knew I was used sexually. I couldn't believe it. Ladies I understand that some of you, if not many of you, have a bucket list of men you want to have sexually. Some of you brought these desires with you from the world and some of you have fantasy lust to have certain men. So ladies, are you a daughter of God? Everything I said about the sons applies to you. There's no point in saying the same information again. Just like there are men with game who purposely sleep with several ladies in their church, women do it too. It's the same game and it's sin.

Marcus L. Boston

The only difference is the ladies are looked down upon most of the time. The men should be looked down upon for this as well. I know all cases are different, but we should all avoid sexual sin and we wouldn't have to worry about this ever happening to us. Have I ever been turned off by finding out a woman had a reputation? Absolutely! Like I mentioned earlier about the brother who had five women, will God give these type of women husbands? Yes. Listen y'all, God will make sure we are equally yoked if He's involved in connecting us. I'm not saying a virgin will get another virgin, but what I'm saying is God is faithful and just. A man who's been thoroughly cleaned up by God, and a woman who's been thoroughly cleaned up by God, are very valuable to the Lord. Ladies and gentlemen, please bring your games and past sexual encounters to God. Bring your horny flesh to God. Seek the Lord and let God clean you up. If we desire God's best we need to be God's best. Let God make us His best for our future spouse. Stop being players sons and daughters of God. If you're sleeping around stop it. Period. This is biblical. "For this is the will of God, even your sanctification, they ye should abstain from fornication: That every one of you should know how to possess his vessel in sanctification and honor; Not in the lust of concupiscence, even as the Gentiles which know not God: For God hath not called us unto uncleanness, but unto holiness." First Thessalonians chapter 4 v. 4, 5, and 7.

Fornication covers everything sexually. Not just intercourse.

You don't believe me do you? Let's look at the word fornication in the blueletterbible.org because the devil has used the English dictionary definition to deceive Christian singles. Most English dictionaries say fornication is unmarried sexual intercourse. So many Christians took this thinking a penis inside a vagina is sin. Therefore we can give and receive oral sex and it's ok. Fornication has three different meanings G1608 *ekporneuō*, G4202 *porneia*, and G4203 *porneuō*. The root word in all three New Testament definitions is "porn." The world of pornography contains everything sexual. Anything you do that brings a sexual orgasm is fornication. It's just like the world of porn. Porn covers everything that brings or gives an orgasm on all spectrums. Put the word porn in place of the word fornication in the bible. How do you feel now? All of you Christians who were doing everything else sexually, how do you feel? You have been deceived by the enemy. All sex before marriage is fornication, it's sin, and it's unclean. God has not called us to uncleanness. Our bodies are the temple of God. "Know ye not that your bodies are the members of Christ? Shall I then take the members of Christ, and make them the members of a harlot? God forbid. What? Know ye not that he which is joined to a harlot is one body? For two, saith he, shall be one flesh. Flee fornication. Every sin that a man doeth is without the body; but he that committeth fornication sinneth against his own body." First Corinthians chapter 6 v. 15, 16 &18. Listen, I didn't like it either.

Let's go further.

Earlier I mentioned being "a real virgin." What's a real virgin? Here's what I said in my book, "I'm Burning. Abstinence Tools For Single Christians" page 27 & 28.

If you're still a virgin reading this book, great! May the Lord keep you and may you flee fornication in Jesus name. Keep your virginity with all diligence and be that pure gift on your wedding night, amen? Amen! Be a real virgin. Don't be deceived by the flesh or deceitful sexual ideas like: "Well, if I only have oral sex I'm still a virgin." "If I have anal sex I'm still a virgin." All of these so called ideas and fleshly philosophies are not of God. If you have not had your penis inside a vagina, but it's been inside a woman's mouth and/or inside her booty hole, and if your mouth has been on a vagina licking, you are not a virgin. The same thing applies to you women who are receiving and giving oral sex, having anal sex, but your vagina has never been penetrated with a penis; you are not a virgin. This is deception. You all have been tricked by the devil. Those very thoughts to do these things came from Satan. Flee fornication truly means to flee all sexual activity. Plus, you are supposed to honor God with your bodies. Those sexual activities do not honor God and they defile your body. If you're guilty, well, repent and cease from it. Ask the Lord to cleanse you of all of those things. Be a real virgin and not a sexually polluted virgin. Amen? Amen! Anything that causes you to achieve or give an orgasm is sex.

Just because you have not had sexual intercourse does not make you a virgin if you've done everything else sexually. You are deceived if you believe you can do all those things and still call yourself a virgin. You're lying to yourself and to those you keep telling you're a virgin.

I know that was pretty graphic for some of you religious folks. Get used to my transparent writing. In the mid 2000s I met a woman of God and she told me she was a virgin. I was so surprised and very curious how she remained a virgin. I wanted to know her story. This would be our only conversation. Although it appeared we were about to start a dating journey, I let this idea go. She was a singer, minister of music, and a pastor's daughter. She assumed I was like the men of God she's been dealing with before. I wasn't ready when she told me if I was her man, she would give me oral sex and anal sex until we got married. She wanted to receive oral sex from me. She believed fornication was vaginal sexual intercourse with a penis, and believed it was ok to do everything else. I couldn't believe my ears. She talked so freely about it like she knew I was going to agree with her. She was very sexually graphic. When I began speaking in vocabulary ending our conversation she quickly responded, "What? It sounds like you're not going to talk to me again." And I didn't. She wasn't a real virgin. She had her hymen, but she received orgasms and given men orgasms. A real virgin is a man or woman who has never had any sex of any kind ever. There's a man of God who used to be a homosexual and now he's a Christian. He told me he was a virgin. I asked, "How are you a virgin?" He replied, "I've never had sex with a woman." I just looked at him. I didn't understand his logic. This man had sex with men. That's still sex. He's not a virgin. If you were gay and now saying you're straight, you're not a virgin if you had sex with the same sex. Please stop the madness. Everything and anything that brings or gives an orgasm is fornication (porn). However you do it, if it brings an orgasm it's sex and sin. We are to live free of fornication. I know and understand how hard it can be for us. Nonetheless, this is the will of God.

Have I ever told any man of God what happened sexually with me and a daughter of God sexually? I wish I could say no. In my books I never use real names or give information to specifically identify anyone. I share my life so everyone will see just how graceful God has been to me in these thirty years. There were times when I was asked if I had sex with certain women of God, and I lied to protect both of us from reproach. I was never a kiss and tell kind of guy in the world, but one specific time I opened my mouth very big at church. Well, here's what happened.

About a week before they were getting married, my ex stopped me after church. We talked briefly. We rarely talked once it was over between us, and now that she was engaged to the pastor's son, we didn't talk at all. The main thing about this conversation I remember was the part that hurt me. She said in a somewhat smug attitude, "I guess you'll make someone a good husband." as she walked off from me. Those words cut me to my core. I immediately walked outside of the church. I saw Minister Jackson and approached him. "What's wrong Brother Marcus? You look like something is bothering you." He asked in a concerned tone. I told him what just happened. As I shared it with him, he responded, "Oh God...... Oh God..... Oh God....." Then I said something that I shouldn't have said to him, "Well, at least there's nothing he can do to her sexually that I haven't done to her already." I uttered those words in a very arrogant attitude. Minister Jackson replied, "Brother Marcus, nooooooo, nooooooooo Brother Marcus. Don't say that. Oh my God!" as he paced back and forth as I talked to him. Then he says, "This whole situation is just wrong. There's no way he should be marrying her. At least let the girl get over you first. She isn't over you and she's marrying him. This isn't right. This isn't right at all." Then I turned around to see the pastor's son and his fiancé exit the church together. Our eyes met just for a second and I didn't turn away at all. He looked away as I continued looking at him. I then fixed my eyes on her, and she did not look in my direction. In that same attitude I had as I talked to Minister Jackson, I started thinking, [She's got some nerve talking about I might make someone a good husband. This dude ain't got a job either. Hell, he's fresh out a prison and a felon. I look way better than this dude. You know what? Why am I trippin' over her? I like women wearing makeup. I like women wearing pants. She's not the woman I loved anyway. The woman I loved is long gone.] Minister Jackson touched my shoulder, "Brother Marcus, calm down! Let it go! Don't let this eat you up. You'll get over her. There will be some other woman for you. It will be alright." [Did he just read my mind or something?] I didn't even respond to Minister Jackson. My mind was still messed up and focused on them. The more I thought about those two, the angrier I got until I got in my mom's car to go home." From Woman To Woman page 208 paragraph 1.

I knew everything my brother in Christ was going to get on his wedding night. Once he knew I thoroughly sexed her he hated me. Everyone knew my ex and I fornicated prior to her meeting the pastor's son. She met him a month after it was over with us. At the time I said this to the minister, the pastor's son already knew we had sex. I was hurt and wanted to get even with her for what she said. I was a full year into my Christian walk when this happened. I was still a babe in the Lord. However, I know single men of God who are on platforms and in positions in the church who are sharing the things they did with women of God. As I'm writing this book, I was informed about another situation involving a single assistant pastor. He is having sex with three different women in his church. There's a big difference from a babe fornicating and a mature Christian. Eli's sons were mature in the word of God. Ladies if you're currently having sex with a man in church leadership, how do you feel about your situation? If you know other women are involved, how do you feel about competing with these women? You're sharing a man of God sexually. Chances are he's not going to pick any of you for marriage. Honestly, would you really want a hoe to be your husband? Just repent and ask God to give you the grace to exit. If you're in an exclusive relationship, or engaged to be married, that's different, but it's still sin. If you're having sex with your pastor, whether he's single or married, you need to seriously exit this situation. You know it's wrong and your pastor knows it's entirely wrong. If your pastor is single, are they trying to marry you? If they aren't talking about marriage move on. You were used sexually. Why are you there? If they're married, and you're the side piece, exit the situation. You were used sexually. Get my book, "What To Do When You Know Your Pastor Is Wrong." All biblical answers to transition out of this situation in a biblical manner. Even if you were played by your pastor, you were still in sin and sin has consequences. We all reap what we sow.

One of the biggest lies I've ever heard is, "It's ok to have sex because we're getting married." I've heard this one several times by different individuals who don't know each other. The sex games are real. Any statement that causes you to sin is not from God. God is not going to give you a stamp of approval to sin against His word. I know of couples who gave each other oral sex prior to marriage, but did not have sexual intercourse. They really believed this was right in the eyes of God. It's still sin people of God. I love sex like most of you reading this book love sex. I know a woman of God who doesn't like sex, but she desires a husband. I was baffled. We went back and forth. The thought of having sex three times a week was too much for her. She said once a month was good. She hasn't even met the man she will marry and her sex life is already planned without his input. Help her Jesus. We kept going back and forth until I came to this conclusion. I finally said, "Well, God is faithful. Maybe God has a man who doesn't like sex just like you and he will cause you both to meet each other." She smiled. It will definitely be God if she meets such a man. She really just wants the companionship and very little sex. Before I change this serious subject let me add this. Apostle Paul actually says that we should not keep company with a brother or sister who are fornicators.

Please read First Corinthians chapter 5. This whole chapter is dealing with some serious issues. This church has a negative sexual sin reputation. There was so much fornication going on and people were arrogant about it. A son slept with his father's wife; his stepmother. Notice only the word fornication is used not adultery. The stepmother committed adultery against her husband, and she wasn't stoned to death with her stepson. They both lived. Times have changed with Israel. God sees you and

God does reveal sinful acts. "This is just between us and God." No it's not. Are you that full of lust that you would do this to your father or mother? The stepparent who sleeps with their stepchildren, and the stepchildren who sleep with their stepparent, are truly in debauchery. In verse 2 the son is arrogant he had his father's wife and doesn't have any remorse. This son is unrepentant. Apostle Paul dealt with this sin. In verse 5 Paul says, "To deliver such a one unto Satan for the destruction of the flesh, that the spirit may be saved in the day of the Lord Jesus." Can you imagine delivering someone to Satan? How is this possible? How exactly is or was this done? No one teaches on this in the church today. Who has the revelation of what this really means? Anyone? If there's a teaching on this that you know of, please message me with the link on social media. I would love to hear it just for information purposes only. It may or may not be a true revelation. When I'm not sure I say it's my opinion. There's so much Apostle Paul had revelation and knowledge about that we don't have today. Apostle Paul says this person will still be saved when Jesus comes. So what does this mean? I believe it means this person will be bound by evil spirits. Bound so much that they are no longer arrogant over what they did, but are now tormented by their sin. Satan can't kill them. Just torment them until they humble themself. Remember when God allowed Satan to have control over Job? Doesn't seem too farfetched now. Could this be the same thing?

It most certainly sounds similar. God gave Satan guidelines and boundary's concerning Job. Most of all, Job did nothing to deserve what he experienced. This son in First Corinthians had sex with his father's wife and bragged about it. Apostle Paul said this son will still be saved. This is a mystery. Only God truly knows how someone is given over to Satan. I believe God removes this person out of our hearts without us being knowledgeable of it. This person will no longer be covered in prayer. I believe no one will be praying or interceding for this person. This person is literally tormented by what they did. They start hating it and start desiring to repent. Maybe some of you players will be given over to Satan, and become bound to a woman who will be your tormentor. You ever wonder why some saints have the craziest drama? Could this be the reason? You played her and now she's destroying your life. You played him now he's stalking you and you're living in fear. Only God truly knows. Just my opinion, but isn't this interesting? Paul did it again! He turned someone over to Satan in the book of First Timothy. I talked about this in my book, "Tainted Influence. Identifying Prophetic Truth & Error." Page 154 – 156 Here's what I wrote.

In the book of First Timothy chapter 1 verses 18 through 20 KJV reads, "This charge I commit unto thee, son Timothy, according to the prophecies which went before on thee, that thou mightest by them war a good warfare; Holding faith, and a good conscience; which some having put away concerning faith have made shipwreck: Of whom is Hy-me-nae'-us and Alexander; whom I have delivered unto Satan, that they may learn not to blaspheme." Wow! Apostle Paul delivered two Christians over to Satan because they blasphemed the Lord. Read it for yourself in your very own bible. In addition, in the book of Second Timothy chapter 2 verses 15 through 18 KJV says, "Study to shew thyself approved unto God, a workman that needeth not to be ashamed, rightly dividing the word of truth. But shun profane and vain babblings: for they will increase unto more ungodliness. And their word will eat as doth a canker: of whom is Hy-me-nae'-us and Phi-le'-tus; Who concerning the truth have erred, saying that the resurrection is past already; and overthrow the faith of some." I really believe Hy-me-nae'-us became a false prophet. This is my opinion people of God. The Apostle Paul said he delivered him over to Satan. Wow! That is amazing! I believe the Apostle Paul stopped praying for him and allowed Satan to have his way in his life. Even as Moses prayed for God to stop His judgment on the children of Israel because of their unbelief and sins, I believe Paul stopped praying for Hy-me-nae'-us because he was misleading the saints of God. God stopped His judgment because of the prayers of Moses, and I believe the prayers of Paul did the same until Paul stopped praying for Hy-me-nae'-us. You never know who's prayers are keeping the Lord's wrath and judgment off of your life; especially when you aren't praying for yourself and/or when you are now in a spirit of error. Let me say that again. When you are in error you never know who's prayers are keeping God's judgment off of your life. This is why God says to pray for our enemies. God doesn't desire anyone's soul destroyed for eternity, but when Paul stopped praying for Hy-me-nae'-us, the mercy Hy-me-nae'-us received through Paul's prayers was removed and Satan attacked Hy-me-nae'-us freely. Hy-me-nae'-us proclaimed that the resurrection had already passed and caused the faith of some to be shattered. Hy-me-nae'-us had a spirit of error which misled him from the spirit of truth. This is why I believe he became a false prophet. He had a few followers who believed the things he taught such as Alexander and Phi-le'-tus, and I'm sure he had more followers who are not mentioned in the bible. When Paul stopped praying for Hy-me-nae'-us, Satan now had free course in his life, and this is why it's good to have a pastoral covering. This was God's judgment on Hy-me-nae'-us. I'm sure Hy-me-nae'-us had space to repent and I'm sure God sent a word of warning to him before Apostle Paul stopped praying for him, but I'm convinced he didn't take heed to it. Now look at the fruit of Hy-me-nae'-us. He caused the saints of God to lose their faith in the Lord. He operated in a spirit of error and false revelations of God's word because he proclaimed the resurrection had already passed when it didn't take place as of yet. As you already read, false prophets operate in error and cause people to lose their souls by false revelations.

(First John Chapter 4 verses 1 through 3) Remember saints of God, if any revelation does not line up with the holy scriptures it is not God's revelation, but man's opinionated error of God's word, or demonic doctrine. Watch as well as pray and know the bible thoroughly in His truth.

Apostle Paul dealt with the sins of the saints. I wish I could talk to Apostle Paul about everything God gave him in revelations. I know he didn't write them all in his epistles. Imagine if we did what Apostle Paul said to do in verse 9 and 11. Verse 9 and 11 says we should not keep company with any Christian who's a fornicator. What's a fornicator? These are the people of God who aren't trying to abstain from sexual sin. They have embraced sexual sin and will not stop. They have absolutely no intention to stop having premarital sex. They're not trying to change. They are not trying to please the Lord. They only want to please themselves. It's all about them and their sexual needs. Their sexual pleasure is above God. It doesn't matter what the Lord asks of them, or what His word says. It doesn't matter if the two of you were together years before you both got saved. It doesn't matter if you're living together and then got saved together. Whatever your excuse is, you are not trying to stop fornicating. Apostle Paul says we shouldn't keep company, hangout, kick it, go out to eat, to the movies, or anywhere else with you type of Christians. I used to have this mindset of trying it out before marriage like many of you. No one wants to live with bad sex in a marriage. Once the Lord allowed me to see this was iniquity in my heart, I repented of it.

Before I complete this chapter, I want to share a very unusual story. On my Facebook and Instagram, I shared a post I first saw on Instagram. It's about a woman of God who married a man of God. This man of God was born without a penis. Yes you read that correctly. My heart went out to this man of God and I cried in prayer for him. I know that brother is broken in ways I will never understand. I couldn't imagine his pain and humiliation. I cried out to God in prayer to supernaturally give this man a penis. I wept for this man of God, "Lord please perform a creative miracle and give this man a penis." This post is dated June 9th, 2023. My heart went out to the woman of God. They fled fornication, but he had every reason to avoid it. She desires to have children. I read many of the comments on the original post. Most said get a divorce. I'm asking God to give him a miracle. However, I believe he should have told her before they got married of his condition. I'm sure he told others and they walked away. Can you imagine living like this? Before you get married, I highly recommend a good thorough sexual conversation. A conversation that doesn't lead to fornication. You don't have to fornicate to find out if you're sexually compatible. Ladies I understand why you want to try it out before marriage. It's still sin. It's very sad that so many God sent spouses never legally became spouses because they chose fornication over obeying God. Have you ever thought, or considered, maybe God didn't want your fornication to be good because it's sin? He's still God while you're fornicating. Your body is still God's temple while you are having sex. God is watching you while you're in sexual sin. As I grew in the Lord during my years of abstinence, God anointed me in many ways. In my book, "From Woman To Woman Volume Three," you see this growth and there were times when I tried to fornicate, and couldn't get in the mood. The marital gift of sex you must receive by faith. If God really brought you two together, He has already considered your bedroom ministry to each other. Do you trust God? Do you love God? Son and daughter, where is your love, respect, and honor toward God and toward each other? So you really believe sinning is really giving you a taste of what your future marriage bed might be? That's if you make it to marriage. You could have just played yourself.

I understand the sexual frustrations with singleness in Christ. I get it. I'm guilty of plenty of fornication. At least I have some years of abstinence under my belt several times. There's one particular woman who I didn't truly write about because we attended the same church and it would have been difficult trying to write about her without people knowing who she is. There are plenty of people who will sue you, if they can, for defamation of character. I talked about her in "From Woman To Woman Volume Three" in the chapter, "The Last Woman." For those who know me, you know exactly who the last woman is. We didn't fornicate before marriage. We didn't do anything that brings about an orgasm prior to marriage. We didn't even kiss until our wedding day after our vows. We were determined to honor God and His word. We were on one accord in this area. Our wedding night was amazing and memorable. I don't believe it could have been any better. Romantic, funny, sexy, and full of lasting intense passion. God was faithful. It's sad our marriage failed. Our wedding night was one of two things that kept me holding on until I knew it wasn't worth fighting for anymore. I stopped believing God for a miracle. During our separation my wife talked about me negatively on social media and I could have sued her for defamation of character. Instead I wrote what really happened with us although it's truly embarrassing. It's not God's fault our marriage failed. God gave me a revelation that caused me to write my book, "For Better or Worse. Why Christians Get Divorced?" No details of my former marriage are in this book, but because of the attack I received on social media, I wrote our story in "From Woman To Woman Volume Three." Prior to marriage she asked me if I dated anyone at our church. Here's what I wrote in "From Woman To Woman Volume Three," in the chapter, "The Last Woman." Page 233 paragraph 1.

She wasn't honest with me about being healed over her sexual Traumas and I wasn't honest with her about one thing. Deep breath in... holding... exhaled. Ok. She asked me before we were engaged if I ever dated anyone from our church. Now, I didn't want to answer this question. I didn't want to give a yes because that yes would lead to more questions. So I said, yes and no. Her response, "Why yes and no?" This was the answer I wanted from her and I hoped she didn't ask any more questions after I answered. I responded, "Well, she no longer attends our church." She did not ask me anymore questions. This was not the exact truth. The truth is this: I did date a woman eighteen years younger than myself, and this relationship is in my book, "Heaven Moves Me." There was another woman I did not date who went to our church. Now, I cannot describe how she looks. I cannot say what she does at church. I cannot give you any information. This woman and I had plenty of sex. Did she leave our church? No comment. Is she active in our church? No comment. Did The Last Woman ever post this woman on her Facebook page? No comment. Does The Last Woman have pictures with this woman on social media? No comment. This was the part of the answer that was "no." We did not date each other although we hung out. It was just sex for a short season, and very good sex I must say. She was like the older woman in volume one.

The whole point I brought this woman up is because this woman knows my ex-wife. Well, she knew her before we got married. How many of us are in situations like this? Sometimes it can be awkward if the sex was good, and if feelings were involved. It was awkward for me once our marriage started being dismantled. Why? Because this woman and I had great sex. As our marriage grew worse, marriage counseling didn't help us. Why did I share this info? If there is anything you know about yourself that could destroy your future marriage, please talk about it before you get married. Talk about the things that could sabotage your wedding vows. Be honest with each other. Get my book, "For Better Or Worse. Why Christians Get Divorced?" for a thorough teaching. It will bless you. You're going to have to talk about the things that are sensitive and uncomfortable about your past. If your past can destroy your future marriage talk about it. Get some therapy, counseling, healing, deliverance, and wholeness before you get married.

Let's complete what I was saying about Apostle Paul. He was instructing us not to keep company with fornicators in the church. Does this seem very judgmental? We shouldn't judge each other huh? Well, Eli didn't judge his sons and God judged him and his sons. Apostle Paul is judging this situation so God is not going to judge Apostle Paul. Eli heard the reports and did nothing. Paul heard the reports and judged the situation. In verse 9 and 11 Paul says don't hangout with fornicators. Apostle Paul wasn't playing with the sins of God's people. Pastors what are you going to do about the whoremongers in your church? Are you going to judge them? Or will God come judge you along with them? Eli did nothing. Will you also do nothing pastor?

For everyone reading this book who has a pure heart, I'm very sure what you just read up to this point was surprising if not shocking. Titus chapter 1 verse 15, "Unto the pure all things are pure: but unto them that are defiled and unbelieving is nothing pure; but even their mind and conscience is defiled." This verse in the book of Titus shows how people with pure hearts see everything pure. This is why players in the church use so many women and men of God; especially those who grew up in the church who have never been in the world. These women are clueless to the game along with some men who grew up in the church. On the contrary, many men and women who grew up in the church learned to play games in the church. Here's how men who grew up in the church become players. (whoremongers) "To deliver thee from the way of the evil man, from the man that speaketh froward things; Who leave the paths of uprightness, to walk in the ways of darkness; Who rejoice to do evil, and delight in the forwardness of the wicked; Whose ways are crooked, and they froward in their paths:" Proverbs chapter 2 v. 12 – 15. Although they are within the church congregation they have left the path of uprightness. God is light and if you're not living for God you're in darkness. "The backslider in heart shall be filled with his own ways:" Proverbs chapter 14 v. 14. All backsliders don't leave the church building or congregation. When men in the church turn their hearts from God their hearts become filled with darkness. Their righteous ways change into crooked ways. Froward means stubbornly contrary and disobedient. These men know they are wrong, but they don't care at this point. God is on the back burner in their lives. Froward means many other things. Look this word up ladies.

There are verses for the ladies as well. "To deliver thee from the strange woman, even from the stranger which flattereth with her words; Which forsaketh the guide of her youth, and forgetteth the covenant of her God. For her house inclineth unto death, and her paths unto the dead. None that go unto her return again, neither take they hold of the paths of life. That thou mayest walk in the way of good men and keep the paths of the righteous." Proverbs chapter 2 v. 16 – 20. Strange women throughout the book of Proverbs are all considered bad girls. They are far from virgins, they cheat on their husbands, and they are very seductive. Proverbs chapter 7 captures a strange woman seducing a man. Please read this entire chapter now. I will only talk about a few verses. "Let not thine heart decline to her ways, go not astray in her paths. For she hath cast down many wounded: yea, many strong men have been slain by her." v. 25 & 26. I shared these verses for the men of God who appear so strong and powerful in the Lord. These verses should help men of God humble themselves. The problem is many men of God yield to these women's ways because they always wanted to have sex with a woman like her. Sex is a powerful act. As single people when we have sex we are defiling the temple of God. Many things happen spiritually while we are in sexual sin. The angels of God that are encamped around us cannot protect us while we are sinning. The devil has access to our souls while we are sinning sexually. There are plenty of Christians who don't believe in soul ties. You already read we become one when we have sex. If you're not legally married to the person you still became one. That's a soul tie. I talk about this in very detailed ways in my book, "I'm Burning." So to those people who do not believe in soul ties, I have a question for you. Who was your best sex partner? The person who just entered your mind, who is this person? Are they still in your life? Are they an ex-lover? Why did they enter your mind? Because it's a soul tie. It's not just a memory. Those love songs attached to your ex-lovers. When you hear those songs, do sexual memories replay to you? There are plenty of things that can bring up soul ties. Perfumes, colognes, restaurants, beaches, and whatever else you did together. Jesus said that which is flesh is flesh, and that which is spirit is spirit. If you received evil spirits from this person, God can remove and cast these out of your life. However, your flesh cannot be cast out. Apostle Paul said when he would do good evil is always present. He was talking about his flesh. Romans chapter 7. Carnality is directly connected to our flesh. The more sexual experiences you sow into your flesh, the more soul ties you possess. Don't believe me? Ok. Who was the best kisser? Who found your pleasure spots on your body? Who was the freakiest? Who was boring? Who was the worse overall? Ladies, which man had the biggest ...?" Men, which woman had the tightest ...?" The people entering your mind are your soul ties. Bring them to God in prayer. All of our sexual needs are based on what we experienced sexually. You may not want that person, or persons, anymore, but you desire the same pleasure you received from them. Your flesh remembers and so does your soul. It's just like a song you haven't heard in years. You still remember all of the words. If you loved sex with that person, or persons, you still remember. Sexual disappointments come from the sexual memories we've sown in fornication, and the person we are currently having sex with isn't measuring up to what we now consider sexual satisfaction. All of that passion we sown in our flesh is still there. When you get horny, what enters your thoughts? Stop playing with me. Hopefully your greatest sex is with your spouse. For many single people this person is probably someone they will never marry. Some of you had more than one person enter your mind. Get my book, "I'm Burning" for a thorough teaching on the subject. Fleeing fornication is serious to the Lord.

You players in the house of God need to repent and turn from your wicked ways. So are you a son of God or not? If you're a son of God, stop using God's daughters. Men if you're helping a daughter financially she doesn't owe you any sexual favors. If you're not helping her with a pure heart keep your money. No sugar daddies in the house of God. Enough is enough. God is watching and you do not want God to judge you. Women of God who are using the men of God, are you God's daughter? Stop it ladies. No sugar mommas either.

To everyone with a pure heart, I pray the Lord gives you very sharp discernment so you're never a victim, or never be a victim again, to these men and women playing games in the church. May God let you see the truth immediately. May God heal your heart over the hurt and make you whole for the real one who's coming. In Jesus name I pray. Amen.

Chapter Two

Yield It To God

Because 2023 has so many more sexual things going on in the world and many people in the church have opened up themselves to these activities, God instructed me to write about this. The bible says, "Marriage is honorable in all, and the bed undefiled: but whoremongers and adulterers God will judge." Hebrews chapter 13 v. 4. All of your whoremonger desires, yield it to God and turn away from them. Repent, humble yourself unto God, and ask God to create in you a clean heart and renew the right spirit within you. Psalm 51. God is very serious. He desires us all to stop committing sexual sin. Whoremongers stop. When I say whoremonger, I'm talking to men and women. Yield your whoredom to God and allow the Lord to clean you up. Allow God to change you. Study your bible and apply it. Sincerely ask God to help you.

There are plenty of sexual things that are made popular in the world these days. There are sex clubs, sex parties, and destinations for sex. Porn is more popular than ever. It was once looked down upon, but with these new age demons released into the world they have made this look promising even to children. I was shielded from many things as a child, but with so many children these days being exposed to sex at an early age, we have children who desire to be porn stars. Children who desire to be strippers. Strip clubs are destination hotspots. I remember strip clubs being looked down on, but these days women take their man to the strip club. Women go to the strip club with their girlfriends and tip strippers. They receive lap dances, but yet these women say they are straight. It's amazing how Satan makes many things that are woman on woman look enticing, sexy, and appropriate to women. Are you straight? Or are these energies, vibes, and spirits slowly opening you up to become lesbians or bi-sexual? Straight women willfully touching other women in erotic ways. Why? It's fun? Why is it fun?

Twerking is out of control now. We called it booty dancing, and women didn't do it for entertainment then. If a woman liked you they twerked with you as you danced with them, or they danced in front of you which said, "Come dance with me. I like you." This window of invitation closed if you didn't accept the invite. Sometimes another guy standing by would dance on her. When she saw it wasn't who she wanted she shut it down by walking away while looking at the man she really wanted. Women didn't twerk for anyone. This generation of women twerk for entertainment and for other women. At most clubs today men and women do not dance with each other. The women are grouped with women and the men are grouped with men. They do not play slow jams or slow dancing music. The women twerk for each other and the men watch. Twerking has crossed over to all nationalities of the women. Every female twerks now it seems. I'm on Snapchat. If you screenshot or screen record on Snapchat, Snapchat notifies the person of what you did. There are things that happen on Snap that doesn't happen on other apps. On Snapchat women twerk to entertain their followers. It's unbelievable. Or they twerk to advertise their private Snapchat or "Only Fans" page. Private Snapchat and Only Fans is an app where women twerk, strip, or do porn to their paying followers. I know some women who have an Only Fans page and they asked me if I would join. I declined.

Female rappers no longer cover up their bodies. I suppose it all started with Lil Kim. The 2 Live Crew also played their part during my generation. They had women twerking/booty dancing in very revealing attire in their videos and concert performances. I'll never forget when they were on The Arsenio Hall Show. The women had on leggings with holes showing their goodies. As the 2 Live Crew became more popular, the United States government banned them. The Explicit Lyrics label on music records, tapes, and compact discs, all started because of the 2 Live Crew xxx lyrics. 2 Live Crew changed everything in rap. Rappers started casting sexy women in their videos. This continued and progressed to where we are today. The female rappers today are also extremely provocative. They twerk with many other women in their videos. Sex and sexual content are everywhere around us these days. God is still God and His word is still His word whether we like it or not.

If you don't believe Jesus is coming something is wrong with you. Same sex couples are kissing and having love scenes on sitcoms and movies. Sex trafficking women and children is popular today. One day a friend and I talked about this. We came to this question: who are the people paying to have sex with these women and children? Somebody is keeping sex trafficking in business. If there were no customers there would be no sex trafficking. If you're a Christian involved in the sex trade, or helping with trafficking, shame on you! If you're paying to have sex with women, children, or both, shame on you! It's sin! Help set those women and children free in the name of Jesus! Amen!!!

For those of you who love multiple sex partners at the same time, you're going to need deliverance, healing, and wholeness from the Lord. The marriage bed is undefiled. However, you can defile your marriage bed. If you're married and you both are bringing outside people in your marriage bed, you are in adultery. Even if you are both in agreement it's still adultery. Your lustful unclean desires God doesn't respect. If you are married and having sex with other married couples, you are in adultery. I tell you so many people are trying to find loopholes in God's word. There are no loopholes. All of these things being done, including the things I've already written, only shows that all parties do not know God like they should, or they know God but do not honor or respect Him. Most of all, it clearly shows they do not love God. There's no way you can love God and do these things knowing God will judge you for it. "Only God can judge me." People who say this are tremendously ignorant of the word of God. Listen if God judges you while you're still alive, you're going to pray for His mercy. It's not going to be a laughing matter. When God judges no one on earth can help you. You don't want to experience this. If you're still alive you have a chance to repent and cry out for mercy. If you're dead and God judges it's too late. If your life didn't reflect Jesus this is going to be a serious problem for you. Our salvation is in Jesus. There is no other salvation. There is no other way to get into heaven. There's Jesus and then there is everything else. Jesus is the way, the truth, and the life. No one goes to the Father except through Jesus. Unfortunately many people will find this out when they are judged by God. Our lives must have the salvation of Christ. "If ye then be risen with Christ, seek those things which are above, where Christ sitteth on the right hand of God. Set your affection on things above, not on things on the earth. For ye are dead, and your life is hid with Christ in God. When Christ, who is our life shall appear, then shall ye also appear with him in glory." Colossians chapter 3 v. 1-4. Read the rest of that chapter. Christ is our life. We yield our entire life unto Jesus. We set out affections on heavenly things. Our former lives are considered dead and hidden with Christ in God. This is why we can't do what we desire to do any longer. We grow in grace by prayer, praise and worship, and studying the word of God. We must allow Jesus to change us through the word of God and His Spirit. His Spirit is a gift we all must receive. If you're a Christian without the Holy Spirit / Holy Ghost, continue to ask God to fill you. You will know when you are filled. Don't just listen to Christians who say you have the Holy Spirit / Holy Ghost. Listen when I was filled there was absolutely no doubt. If you're at a church that teaches you how to speak in tongues, this is not God. I didn't need anyone to tell me I had the Holy Spirit or teach me to speak in tongues. If you don't have the Holy Spirit, ask God to help you receive His gift. You may have a closed spirit like I had. Here's how I was filled with the Holy Ghost / Holy Spirit.

In the summer of 1996, on a Thursday, I was praising God with the fruit of my lips as I washed my dishes. I was telling the Lord how good He was when I suddenly felt something I never felt before. I knew it was the presence of God. I can't explain how I knew it was the Lord, but I knew it was Him. When He entered my kitchen, I became silent as I felt tingles all over my body. That's when I heard His voice softly say to me, "Let me in." I was hysterical and kept saying repeatedly, "OH, COME ON IN LORD, COME ON IN LORD!..." The Lord then said softly, "Shhhhh. Let me in." Again, I said loudly the same words and God repeated, "Shhhhh. Let me in." After taking a deep breath and calming myself down, I humbly replied, "God..., I don't know how to let you in, but will you help me let you in?" I felt the Lord and myself together open my spirit and God filled me with the Holy Ghost. I began to speak in tongues for the first time ever in my life. What an awesome experience I had with the Lord that evening. Since that day, I had beautiful communion with the Lord. I started praising the Lord longer and studying my bible longer. Eventually, I spent so much time with God that my television stayed off. I turned off the ringer on my phone. I didn't want to be disturbed when I spent time with the Lord. Sometimes I worshipped and praised my savior for hours. These hours seemed like a few minutes. I was enjoying my time with the Lord and it was so much better than when I wasn't filled with God's Spirit. A Pastor's Mistake. Page 16 paragraph 3.

I had a closed spirit because of all the hurt, pain, and disappointments of life. It's the equivalent of having walls up and not letting anyone inside. God doesn't force Himself inside of us. We have to willfully let Holy Spirit / Holy Ghost inside of us. Do what I did. Ask God to help you receive Him inside of your spirit. This happened before Church Girl and I fornicated. I'll share this as well. If you do not have the Holy Spirit / Holy Ghost, you do not have the authority of Jesus on your life. Here's what I wrote in my book, "Enchantment. How Witches Attacked Me!" page 105 – 107.

1st John chapter 4 verse 4 says, "Ye are of God, little children, and have overcome them: because greater is he that is in you, than he that is in the world." When you are filled with the Holy Spirit/Ghost, you have the Spirit of truth within you. The Holy Spirit is the power of the living God inside of your spirit. The Holy Spirit will lead you and guide you into all truth. When you are filled with the Holy Ghost, satan knows your name and will attack you as often as he can in some manner. You never want to engage the enemy if you do not have the Holy Spirit. In Acts chapter 19 verses 13 - 16, "Then certain of the vagabond Jews, exorcists, took upon them to call over them which had evil spirits the name of the Lord Jesus, saying, We adjure you by Jesus whom Paul preacheth. And there were seven sons of one Sceva, a Jew, and chief of the priests, which did so. And the evil spirit answered and said, Jesus I know, and Paul I know; but who are ye? And the man in whom the evil spirit was leaped on them, and overcame them, and prevailed against them, so that they fled out of that house naked and wounded." The seven sons of Sceva had no power, no authority, and no identity in Christ. Demons know you when Christ lives in you. You never want to engage any demon without the identity of Christ on your life.

One thing is certain for mature Christians, we engage in spiritual warfare. Ephesians chapter 6 and Second Corinthians chapter 10. My identity is in Christ because my life is hidden in Christ. Therefore His authority is on my life. I have the keys of the kingdom. I can bind and loose in the name of Jesus. Satan knows who I am because I'm serious about my walk with Christ.

I am pressing toward the mark for the prize of the high calling of God in Christ Jesus. Does Satan know your name? Or is he saying, who are you? If you do not have the Holy Ghost, you have no authority and the enemy does not know your name. If you received Jesus sincerely, the gift of the Holy Spirit is promised to you. Receive your promise. In your case, the devil would love to keep you from receiving your gift. Seek the Lord and ask God to help you receive His Holy Spirit. For the people of God who are fornicators and not trying to stop, you have no authority because you are living in unrepentant sin. You're still living in sin although you're going to church. You're not a threat at all to the enemy. As a matter of fact, you are your own enemy. "The merciful man doeth good to his own soul: but he that is cruel troubleth his own flesh." Proverbs chapter 11 v. 17.

Let's continue. Like I was saying we grow in grace by studying the bible, prayer, and praise and worship. As we grow our lives are changed, and we grow from glory to glory. Glory meaning reaching new levels in Christ. The people around you will say one day, "You've changed." It happened to me. Keep your focus on the Lord. As the Lord changes us we reflect the life of Christ. Anytime we commit any sin we must ask for forgiveness and repent quickly. Some of us have strongholds. These are areas of our lives where our sins are extremely hard to break. Yield these areas to God in prayer. Stop saying, "I can't change." Yield it to God and let God make the changes for you, but you must yield it unto God. Yield means to surrender and to give up to another. Let go of your desires God says are sin. In this case we are talking about sexual sin. You can't bring people into your marriage bed. You can't marry more than one spouse like in the Old Testament. Same sex is sin. Bi-sexual life is sin. To all of you lgbtq stop saying God created you this way. If you really feel this way, are you a son or daughter of God? Or the lowercase god the devil? Yield all of your lgbtq desires, personalities, ideals, feelings, ways unto God, and allow Him to change you. God loves us all, but there are no heaven guarantees. We must surrender all of us to Jesus. We all want to hear well done my good and faithful servant. Only the pure at heart shall see God. Every desire we have that is against God's word is inside our hearts. Therefore our hearts are not pure. Our hearts are defiled. "For out of the heart proceed evil thoughts, murders, adulteries, fornications, thefts, false witness, blasphemies: These are the things which defile a man: but to eat with unwashen hands defileth not a man." Matthew chapter 15 v. 19 - 20. We all shall be judged according to our deeds, and if any area of our lives are not hidden in Christ, we will be in trouble. We want God to see the blood and life of Jesus covering our lives. If God sees us we will be in trouble. If you think any sin is going to make it into heaven you are clearly wrong. Whoremongers, fornicators, adulterers, and lgbtq are not going to heaven. Why? It's sin, and all sexual sin defile our bodies and our bodies are the temple of God. "If any man defile the temple of God, him shall God destroy; for the temple of God is holy, which temple ye are." First Corinthians chapter 3 v. 17.

So I talked with another woman of God during a break from writing this book. She was telling me about the men of God sending her pics of their penis. Fortunately for her this turns her off. We had a very long conversation and I ended up praying for her. Pure women of God desire men of God to be pure. Not lustful and disrespectful. I'm glad she was turned off. However, I suppose some women of God are turned on. Daughters if you love receiving these types of pics, yield it to God. If you're lusting to see what you can do with a man's penis, or what a man can do with it, yield it to God. Men yield it to God. Men and women of God stop sexting. You never know who these pics will be shared with in the future. A brother in Christ showed me a pic I wasn't ready to see. I wasn't prepared when he showed me a naked woman of God. I asked him, "Where did you get that?" Another brother in Christ sent it to him. Please stop sexting. Can you imagine you're engaged to be married, and a bitter ex-sends your fiancé naked pics or a sex video starring you? Repent and cease from it. You can't change your past, but you can look well to your future. Again, talk about the things that could destroy your future marriage. I talk about sexting in my tell-all books. Yield these desires and ways unto the Lord. Seek God's face. Read your bible. Exactly how you talk to your best friend talk to

God in prayer. Be honest with the things in your heart. Here's something to remember: God's word and God's voice will always agree. If you hear any voice telling you to do something that's against the written word of God, well, that's not God talking to you. It's a false voice. It's an evil spirit trying to deceive you.

If you love porn, yield it to God. If you love raping women and men, yield it to God. If you're a child molester, yield it to God. Reject all of these desires and deeds, renounce these desires and deeds, repent for doing these things, and allow God to cleanse you. Pray for those you raped and molested to be healed and made whole. If you love having sex with dead bodies, yield it to God. If you love having sex with animals, yield it to God. Incest, family sex, sex with stepchildren, and sex with stepparents, yield it to God. Bring all of your sex addictions and fetishes to God. This goes for everything in our lives. If you're into the nastiest of desires, yield them to God. Your body is the temple of the living God. We should not be doing anything that defiles our bodies according to the word of God. This is why seeking God's face helps us. The more the Lord changes our hearts, and the desires of our hearts, the more our affections become the desires the Lord approves. Learn to love giving God praise and worship. Fall in love with God. You will eventually get to a place where you sincerely desire to please the Lord. Grow in grace. If you sin in any kind of way, ask for forgiveness, and stick with the Lord. Don't worry about what people are going to say about you. Best believe they have sinned too. Go boldly before the throne of grace and keep learning the bible. Keep praying and seeking the Lord. Amen. God created one man to be married to one woman. The marriage bed is one man and one woman; no one else. There aren't any other marriage beds recognized by God that He honors and blesses. If your marriage bed are two men, or two women, it's sin. As a matter of fact, God doesn't recognize your man-made marriage as the marriage institution He created. Only what God has established does He recognize.

Did you know that there's a gangbang in the bible? For those of you who don't know, a gangbang is when a bunch of men all have sex with the same woman at the same time. Every orifice of the woman is used for sexual pleasure all at the same time, along with her hands being used to provide sexual pleasure. In porn all participants had physicals and std tests prior to filming. The woman read the contract before signing it. The men involved also have contracts. These porn stars may already know each other from working in the porn industry together. The woman knows exactly what's about to happen to her during filming. Even though this sex scene looks brutal, and abusive, it's a controlled environment. Everyone is in agreement with what's happening. The woman embraced it before filming started. Her mind, will, and emotions have already been prepared. What you are about to read in the bible is an uncontrolled situation. The woman is not in agreement and I'm sure she wasn't prepared. As a matter of fact, she had no say so at all.

"So he brought him into his house, and gave provender unto the asses: and they washed their feet, and did eat and drink. Now as they were making their hearts merry, behold, the men of the city, certain sons of Belial, beset the house round about, and beat at the door, and spake to the master of the house, the old man, saying, Bring forth the man that came into thine house, that we may know him. And the man, the master of the house, went out unto them, and said unto them, Nay, my brethren, nay, I pray you, do not so wickedly; seeing that this man is come into mine house, do not this folly. Behold, here is my daughter a maiden, and his concubine; them I will bring out now, and humble ye them, and do with them what seemeth good unto you: but unto this man do not so vile a thing. But the men would not hearken to him: so the man took his concubine, and brought her forth unto them; and they knew her, and abused her all the night; until the morning: and when the day began to spring, they let her go." Judges chapter 19 v. 21-25

Doesn't this passage sound familiar? It reminds me of what happened with Lot in the book of Genesis. This situation caused a war between the tribes of the children of Israel. Brothers against brothers. If you read further you will see this woman died from the abuse she received sexually. We do not know the number of men, but the men surrounded the house. The word beset means to attack from all sides, to trouble persistently; harass, to hem in; surround. There were a lot of men. The man of the house only brought his guests concubine, he didn't bring his daughter. He knew what those men were going to do. Maybe his guest agreed the concubine would go alone. Nevertheless, my heart goes out to this concubine. They literally sexed her to death. This was a very brutal sexual act that took place. The things that really gets me is that an old man participated. Was the old man the leader of that mob? Those men really wanted the man. They wanted to abuse him sexually all night. If you're a man of God, old or young, who forcefully comes on to men and women sexually, yield it to God.

Men and women of God, are you a victim of rape or being forcefully handled sexually in the church? Was your circumstance overlooked and disregarded? Bring your pain, hurt, shame, and trauma to God. Call the police. I don't care who told you not to press charges. Read the rest of this chapter and continue reading into the next chapter. Like I said earlier, a war happened with Israel because of what happened with this woman. The tribes fighting for her justice lost the first two battles, but still won the war after the third battle. Pressing charges might be a fight depending on who's involved and people telling you just let God deal with it. Here's what I shared in my book, "A Pastor's Mistake." Page 355

When the service was over, I thought I was about to go home. Then to my astonishment Pastor Davis announced, "We are having an emergency meeting immediately after church today. All members of this church are to be present." I sat in the very back of the church because I wanted to see everything and everyone as the meeting took place. The meeting began once all the visitors exited the church and I was very attentive when Pastor Davis started talking. He stated, "I'm having this meeting because I am sitting down a person from their office. I won't say exactly why, but this individual will no longer have the authority to counsel anyone and cannot operate in this church with the influence they once had (He then said that person's name)." I couldn't believe this person was sat down and I couldn't imagine the reason why. Pastor Davis continued talking by adding, "Now, I will focus more on my family, more now than ever before. I give so much of my time and my life to this ministry. Now, I have to focus on my home and spend more time with my family. (Sister Carmen was nodding in agreement.) While trying to help this church the enemy hit my house." There were many people saying amen as Pastor Davis talked. I sat in silence trying to figure out what was going on. Then Pastor Davis made a comment that really startled me. He loudly and boldly voiced, "MY DAUGHTER IS STILL A VIRGIN!!!" I was sitting in the back of the church thinking to myself, [My daughter is still a virgin? No..., no..., no.... I know that person didn't molest

Pastor Davis' daughter. It couldn't be.] I couldn't imagine that person molesting a child.

In my thirty years of being a Christian, I've seen many offences. Some of which are criminal. I've already talked about a real virgin. This daughter is no longer a real virgin. The only thing I can say of a certainty is that she still has her hymen. This situation really happened and I changed all names of everyone involved. In addition, I purposely excluded information that would make it easy to identify this person. Entire families left this ministry. This also happened at another church where I was a member. I believe I can safely say it's happened at many other churches. One of these two churches had charges filed, and one had the charges dropped. When I say I understand the complexities when crimes are committed by Christians, I mean it. God says don't suffer as an evil doer. Suffer meaning you're punished in prison. "But let none of you suffer as a murderer, or as a thief, or as an evildoer, or as a busybody in other men's matters." First Peter chapter 4 v. 15. Well, if it was my daughter, my sister, or family member who was molested or raped, I would be calling the police. Yes I call police. Like I was saying, if you are the victim of rape file charges. I don't care if it's the pastor. God is not in agreement with these secret criminal sins being concealed because you don't want your church to look bad. So you people who know someone has gotten away with rape or child molestation, how do you feel knowing you're helping a criminal? If they repented that's good, but that's not enough. Own up to what you did. Confess it and turn yourself into the police. I know what I'm saying, and I know many of you aren't going to do this. However, there is a God who's going to deal with this. So many people are angry at God because of sexual crimes committed against them in the church. God didn't do it. Please stop being angry at God. We all have a will of our own. We are all free to make our own choices. There are people in the church who choose to do evil things. They are evil doers. I'm very sure God tried to prevent it. Here's what I said in my book, "What To Do When You Know Your Pastor Is Wrong." Page 93

Parents, if your child was molested by a pastor, or anyone, don't hesitate to call your local authorities. The only way pastors who are guilty of these sins are going to truly stop is if they all start going to prison. Also know it is not God's fault that the pastor, or anyone else, molested your child. Every one of us has a free will to make our own decisions. I'm sure the Lord was speaking to the pastor to not do such an evil thing. Please don't blame the Lord for the situation. Seek God for the answers you are looking for. Meanwhile pray for your child to be healed and purified of what happened. Your child will also need deliverance as well. You will also need to seek the Lord for new direction for you and your child.

I pray the Lord heals all of you who were raped and molested in the church. Forgive yourself if necessary and get some help.

Get therapy, counseling, and deliverance for yourself / for your child. File charges. If you didn't get a rape kit still press charges. Even if this person is not convicted, at least start the paper trail so that if they do it again, the next victim will have your paperwork to be a witness to their situation. If your church isn't standing with you file charges anyway.

There are victims of rape in the bible. King David's daughter Tamar was raped by her brother in Second Samuel chapter 13. In the book of Genesis chapter 34, Jacob's daughter Dinah was raped. Both of these documented events didn't end well. How could rape end well? Maybe the answer is justice. Tamar was hated by her brother after he raped her. Many terrible things happened in David's family following Tamar's rape. Dinah on the other hand, the man who raped her wanted to marry her after he raped her. Two of Jacob's sons, Simeon and Levi, killed the man who raped their sister. (Please don't kill anyone. Call the police.) Read both chapters and see how it ends for each family. Well, I've had many women tell me how someone in their own family raped them. I considered writing a book called, "That's What She Told Me." I can't believe so many women were molested and raped in their own families. Not one of them told anyone in their family, but they told me. I'm still baffled by this. Ladies I pray you all can be at liberty to share what happened to you.

Pastors if you know men are raping women in your church,

BE CAREFUL WITH GOD'S DAUGHTER

you know what you need to do. Call the police. "But let none of you suffer as a murderer, or as a thief, or as an evildoer, or as a busybody in other men's matters." First Peter chapter 4 v. 15. I know I repeated this verse. Peter was telling the body of Christ not to do anything that would cause them to go to prison. If you're a rapist you need to go to prison. I don't care who you are. You're abusing people and think it's ok. Man up and admit what you did. Ask God for the grace to do your prison time. I said the exact same thing in my book, "What To Do When You Know Your Pastor Is Wrong." Page 92 & 93.

To you pastors who are pedophiles and child molesters, humble yourself, repent, ask God for forgiveness, and sincerely seek deliverance. God says, "But let none of you suffer as a murderer, or as a thief, or as an evildoer, or as a busybody in other men's matters. Yet if any man suffer as a Christian, let him not be ashamed; but let him glorify God on this behalf." (First Peter chapter 4 verses 15 through 16) If you committed this crime you will be locked up for your abominations with children. The silence of these children is about to be broken and they are going to expose you perverted pastors. Once you are exposed, you and your ministry will be shamed before the body of Christ. Now you are about to suffer as an evildoer. Ask God for the grace to do your prison time. Parents, if your child was molested by a pastor, or anyone, don't hesitate to call your local authorities. The only way pastors who are guilty of these sins are going to truly stop is if they all start going to prison. Also know it is not God's fault that the pastor, or anyone else, molested your child. Every one of us has a free will to make our own decisions. I'm sure the Lord was speaking to the pastor to not do such an evil thing. Please don't blame the Lord for the situation. Seek God for the answers you are looking for. Meanwhile pray for your child to be healed and purified of what happened.

Like I said earlier, I don't care who you are. If you're guilty of crimes worthy of prison, may God give you the grace to do your prison time. Report these crimes. God is not in agreement with covering up sex crimes. Either we are the children of the living God or we are the children of the devil. Our churches should not be full of wickedness. When you stand before God, what are you going to say? Men of God who are physically beating your wives, what are you going to say? Women who are sexually abusing and molesting young children, what are you going to say? Where will you spend eternity? Yield all of your sins, abuse, lust, whoredom, and sex crimes unto the Lord. Come boldly before the throne of grace. As horrible as these sins are Jesus died for all sin. Jesus died for rapist, child molesters, murderers, etc. Repent. Yield it to God. Seek the face of God and let Him change you from glory to glory. Jeffrey Dahmer received Christ in prison before he was killed. You can search the internet for more information. Jesus died for all sins. Even those things most of us would call unforgivable SIN. I'm sure it is not easy to forgive the people who committed evil against you, but ask God to help you forgive them. "For if ye forgive men their trespasses, your heavenly Father will also forgive you: But if ye forgive not men their trespasses, neither will your Father forgive your trespasses." Matthew chapter 6 v. 14 & 15. If you're having a hard time forgiving, ask God to help you forgive them. There are some victims refusing to forgive their offenders. Once again I understand. However, where you spend eternity depends on your ability to forgive. Ask God for the grace to forgive your offenders. I'm sure it's not easy at all. If the offenders repent sincerely, Jesus will forgive them. Can you forgive?

Men and women of God, sons and daughters, whatever the sins are in your life, yield them to God. From character flaws to sexual sins to sex crimes, yield them unto God. Surrender them willfully. It's time to allow Jesus to shape you and mold you into His image. Renounce your sins and strongholds in your life, and yield them to God. Allow the Lord to transform you from glory to glory. I by the Holy Ghost have named many things in this book. If you want God to judge you continue in sin and you will see that God's grace will not continue to abound. God sees phony repentance. Humble yourself. Sincerely repent. Turn your heart to the Lord. If not, at some point God will judge you for continuing in sin. It's time to speak up about the secret things that happened to you. I bind the spirit of silence in the name of Jesus. Let your voice come forth with boldness and without fear.

Marcus L. Boston

Be courageous in the name of Jesus.

It's amazing how God sees things. One thing is certain, we are all valuable in Christ thanks to his sacrifice on the cross. No matter what walk of life we come from we are valuable to the Lord. This is why He died for all of our sins, He died for all abominations, and He died for all the things we have deemed as unforgivable. God is asking us to yield all of our sins to Him. Will you honor God's word? Or will you continue in sin hoping the grace of God will abound? If you can't stop sinning sexually you need to get married and be faithful to your opposite sex spouse. Whatever your faults, weaknesses, or sins, yield them to God and seek His face. Our bodies are the temple of the living God. Stop defiling your body and stop defiling other people's bodies. Eternity is at stake.

Chapter Three

The New Man Exhortation

People of God, this chapter will help you with your character. Now I am not a fan of anyone being phony. I hate acting phony and being fake. I used to be in the pastor's office every week for a season because of something I said to someone. I had to learn how to talk and communicate in a polite manner. This was the first flaw I had as a new Christian. This was not an easy task for me. I was keeping it real. I didn't know any other way to talk. If you said something I didn't like, well, you knew it. I grew tired of being rebuked by the pastor every week. I didn't know how to talk in a Christian way. The only man I knew was the old man. I was unaware a new man could exist. I had a girlfriend and I was sexually active. Abstinence was very hard for me. What's your excuse if you grew up in the church? Maybe you are in a carnal church. Maybe you are in a religious church. Maybe your church didn't teach you biblical character. I understand that every church is not the same. Some churches don't believe in speaking in tongues. Some churches don't believe in prophecy. Some churches don't believe in women preachers. Some churches don't teach on seeking God, and some churches never preach or teach against sin. Some of you reading this book are shocked. Some of you never knew these things were written in the bible. I don't understand why pastors refuse to teach certain things in the bible. If you don't believe or teach the entire bible, are you a partial son or daughter? Are you halfway on the road to heaven? Is God your half Father? Are you all in, or not? When I was in the world I was looking for God. I didn't believe the bible. The Christians who were around my life weren't good examples. I fought against Christians and debated with them often. In my search for God I ended up getting into Yoruba and ancestral worship. I talk about this in my book, "Running Through The Darkness." The subtitle is, "The Story I Don't Want to Share." I died at the age of 22 and I went to hell. Hell is a very real place. I talk about that experience, Yoruba and ancestral worship intimately in this book. How did I become a Christian? Here's what I shared in my book, "Running Through The Darkness." Page 105 paragraph 1.

How did I become a Christian? Karen (My friend and her husband is one of my best friends) became a Christian and asked me to drop her off at a bible study. I agreed. I planned to go to a party that night that Karen was unaware of. When I dropped her off, she asked me if I wanted to come in. I declined. But, I heard a voice say "Go Inside." I started looking around and followed her inside an apartment; not a church. When I entered this apartment, we were greeted by everyone.

There was a conversation that was taking place that immediately grabbed my attention. This woman was telling her dream to another woman. I was paying attention to every detail. I finally interrupted her and repeated the details of her dream that she had already shared. Then I began to ask did a, b, and c, happen next. She said it did. Then I asked if d, e, f, happen next and her eyes got so big. She almost yelled, "You're the guy in my dream!" I replied, "And you're the woman in my dream." Everyone was in awe at what just took place. This woman and I had the same dream of each other. This is the only time I've ever had a dream of anyone and met them, and learned that they had the same dream about me. This dream talk kept me there longer than I planned on being there. The preacher was late, and as I got up to leave, he was walking in. He asked me to stay and I did. He preached some message on Adam and Eve. I personally didn't believe anything he just preached on. Remember, I don't believe the bible at this time.

This preacher began talking to me and declared, "There's something you're looking for, and you're going to find it. You wanted to be at some party tonight, but God brought you here. (My eyes stretched wide because no one knew about the party I wanted to go to but me.) That wasn't a man in your closet when you were a little kid, that was a demon assigned to destroy your life. (My eyes stretched wider because that was the truth. I used to tell my mom there was a man in my closet and he's trying to get me.) You see what I'm doing, you're going to be doing it too." He said a lot more about my personal life that I won't add.

That information might be in future books. Nonetheless, I looked at the bible someone let me use for that bible study and said in my thoughts, [This bible is for real!] No one at this bible study led me to Christ on this night. I went home and gave my life to Jesus alone, but I didn't know the bible, I didn't understand the bible, and only knew what the church taught me."

Amen! I understand many churches do not teach certain subjects. Your job is to "Study to show thyself approved unto God, a workman that needeth not to be ashamed, rightly dividing the word of truth." Second Timothy chapter 2 v. 15. Regardless of what your pastor is teaching your assignment is to seek the face of God. As we seek God's face, God begins to change our hearts and as our hearts become pure before the Lord, our character begins to reflect the fruit of the Spirit. We begin to live our lives according to God's word. Jesus said, "But seek ye first the kingdom of God, and his righteousness; and all these things shall be added unto you." Matthew chapter 6 v. 33. How do we seek the kingdom of God? Learn about Jesus. Study Matthew, Mark, Luke, and John. Then read the book of Acts and the epistles of Apostle Paul. Learn of the things that please God in His word and ask God to help you live His word. When we seek God first He adds those things that we need in our lives. God desires to be first. So many times we seek everything else and God is last in our lives. Put God first and keep Him first. You may struggle in some areas of your life, but keep seeking God.

Cry out to God for help. This is why we have grace. Grace is for the growing pains of Christianity. You're not going to be perfect, but as you seek the Lord you'll grow and become better in the Lord. Your character will change. How you talk and conduct yourself will change. Don't be phony. Allow God to make these changes in your heart and your actions will change. Allow God to make changes in your heart and the intent of your heart will change. You must seek the Lord. This is the only way you're going to change. If you're not seeking God you're not going to become better in the Lord. "God made me like this and He understands." Did God make you like that? Or did sin form you into the person you are? Well, God desires to change you according to His word. If all of us singles would seek God we would see so many more marriages. For example, at this present time I'm writing this book, I'm not dating and I'm abstinent. I've been legally divorced since September 2021. The last time I had sex was with my wife. I have no desire to be caught up in sin. Women are in my direct messages from time to time, but I'm good. I honestly don't value how fine a woman is anymore. I could care less about all of your curves. I've had sexy curvaceous women. Their beauty didn't help me. Through hurt, pain, and heartbreak have I found what matters to me the most. How I'm treated is very important to me. I'm just as valuable. It's about both of us or I don't want you. You're not a queen and I'm your servant. I'm not beneath you. I'm not a peasant. I'm a king. We are both royalty and we both shall treat each other as royalty or I don't want you. I'm happy with Jesus. I'm not desperate for a wife. I would love to be married again. Here's my concerns. For me to get married again, I have to know that I love her as Christ loves the church, and she must respect me. I can't do drama. I hate arguments. I hate being yelled at. If you can't talk to me without yelling, clapping your hands, and screaming, it can wait until you can talk to me in a proper tone of voice. She has to let me freely be myself. I will let her freely be herself. I've been through too much. Ladies if I ever approach you and you're not interested, please say you're not interested. I'm not going to be mad. I'm going to give God the praise and keep it moving. If you men and women of God desire to be married seek the Lord. Make time for God and you to spend time together. As much as I love the female anatomy and all the sexual pleasures from it, I'd rather be alone if we are going to be the best of enemies. I can't do drama. I will pack up and leave. I'm not living in a stress filled home. I love peace. I love quiet. I love togetherness. I love unity. I can't do fighting. I can't. I won't. I am a new man in Christ Jesus. If it's not kingdom I don't want it. What is kingdom? We are God's children right? "For the kingdom of God is not meat and drink; but righteousness, and peace, and joy in the Holy Ghost. Let us therefore follow after the things which make for peace, and things wherewith one may edify another." Romans chapter 14 v. 17 & 19. I need a wife who loves righteousness, peace, joy, and things that edify. Edify means to encourage intellectual, moral, or spiritual improvement. Plus she must love to dance and love to have fun. Caribbean music is my favorite. Let's continue.

In order for us to become a new man in Christ, we must allow the Lord to change us. You've already read to seek the Lord, pray, spend time with God, study the bible, and yield all of yourself to Christ. Here are some verses to study. "Let this mind be in you, which was also in Christ Jesus." Philippians chapter 2 v.5. Our thought life is very important as it pertains to the new man. Study the life of Jesus in the scriptures. Jesus was full of compassion. This is a great quality to have as a Christian. Some of us are so critical and judgmental toward each other. Ask God to help you have the mind of Christ. As a single Christian, do all you can to avoid having sexual thoughts and fantasies fill your mind. For most of us, these thoughts stir up our flesh and for some of us, it makes us want to make that phone call for sexual gratification. Ask God to help you think on good things outside of sex. "Finally, brethren, whatsoever things are true, whatsoever things are honest, whatsoever things are just, whatsoever things are pure, whatsoever things are lovely, whatsoever things are of good report; if there be any virtue, and if there be any praise, think on these things." Philippians chapter 4 v. 8. "And Jesus said, Somebody hath touched me: for I perceive that virtue is gone out of me." Luke chapter 8 v. 26. We as Christians acquire virtue by spending time with God in His presence. Have you ever prayed for someone and afterwards felt tired or exhausted? I have. Virtue leaves us as we do the work of the Lord. No time with God equals no virtue. This verse explains if we have virtue think on these things. Virtue is a fruit of seeking God. Virtue is a God quality we can only receive from Him. Virtue helps us in many ways as Christians. Virtue is strength, it's help, and so much more. The lady who touched Jesus was healed by faith causing virtue to leave Jesus. Although Jesus is The Son of God, He is our example because He was also flesh. If we follow His example we can do the things Jesus did when He was on the earth in a physical body. Jesus even said, "he that believeth on me, the works that I do shall he do also; and greater works than these." John chapter 14 v. 12. In order for us to do what Jesus did and greater, we must seek His face and believe. Our lives must be hidden in Christ so His life becomes our life. Jesus is our example. Read Matthew, Mark, Luke, and John about Jesus. How much do you want this? Do you believe? As I just typed those words, God is saying this to me as well. I'm in tears. God is so real. Whatever flaws and issues we possess it's not God's fault. We have sin natures, some of us have curses, and bloodline curses that have shaped us into who we are outside of Christ. We have to willfully yield our lives to Christ and seek God so He can change us for His glory. No one is just going to heaven. Jesus said, "I go to prepare a place for you." John chapter 14 v. 2 & 3.

If your life is not hidden in Christ is there a place for you? Let's continue. Our thought life is very important in our walk with Christ. You will get better if you seek God, but you must seek Him. God isn't going to force you. You'll receive virtue in His presence and you will grow in the grace of God. Amen. As we seek the Lord our minds are purged and cleanse by the Lord Himself. We start setting our thoughts and focus on the things of God that are pure, honest, just, lovely, and of a good report. Notice that verse also said if there be any praise. Learn to love praising the Lord. Praise God because He is God and because He deserves it. It's not based on your emotions, feelings, or your circumstances. Praise Him because it's right and in His presence is the fulness of joy. In His presence is His virtue.

Earlier in this book I talked about receiving the Holy Spirit / Holy Ghost. Here are more benefits of having God's Spirit. "Grace and peace be multiplied unto you through the knowledge of God, and of Jesus our Lord, According as his divine power hath given unto us all things that pertain unto life and godliness through the knowledge of him that hath called us to glory and virtue: Whereby are given unto us exceeding great and precious promises: that by these ye might be partakers of the divine nature, having escaped the corruption that is in the world through lust." Second Peter chapter 1 v. 2 – 4. I appreciate these verses because they remind us that God's grace is multiplied unto us through the knowledge of God. This confirms what I've been saying throughout this book. Seek the Lord and study your bible. As you seek God you receive more grace as you grow. Read Second Peter chapter 1 v. 5 – 9. This is a recipe to grow in God by His grace. You keep adding more and more of God in your life. Verse 3 says through the knowledge of Him who called us to glory and virtue. The Holy Spirit / Holy Ghost is God's divine power and His divine nature. His power and nature is now inside of us in our spirit. As we grow in Him we will be changed from the old man into the new man in Christ Jesus. Verse 4 says that we escaped the corruption that is in the world through lust. Apostle Paul wrote this almost two thousand years ago. Is lust worse today? Not at all. It's the same lust. The difference is that we have more technology for lust to be seen globally. Remember a son slept with his father's wife and bragged about it. They were fornicators and cheaters. They loved sex just like we do and risked being stoned to death unlike us. They were being corrected by Apostle Paul by epistles and those same epistles are helping our Christian walks today.

We just read about escaping lust. Here is a verse that contains several different words that describe lust. "Mortify therefore your members which are upon the earth; fornication, uncleanness, inordinate affection, evil concupiscence, and covetousness, which is idolatry: For which things sake the wrath of God cometh on the children of disobedience: In the which ye also walked some time; when ye lived in them. But now ye also put off all these; anger, wrath, malice, blasphemy, filthy communication out of your mouth. Lie not one to another, seeing that ye have put off the old man with his deeds; And have put on the new man, which is renewed in knowledge after the image of him that created him." Colossians chapter 3 v. 5 - 10. Do a study on these scriptures. For some of you reading this book I know this is a lot. Take a deep breath. In order to overcome your hormones, your flesh, and fornication, you're going to need spiritual ammunition. It's going to be a battle. I'm not saying you'll never fornicate again. I'm saying keep seeking God no matter what happens. At some point victory will be yours. At some point your mind will be made up to stand, but it's going to take God's grace and virtue to do it. If you're in doubt right now as I was as a new Christian, seek the Lord. Your old man will get weaker and the new man will get stronger.

"Put on therefore, as the elect of God, holy and beloved, bowels of mercies, kindness, humbleness of mind, meekness, longsuffering; Forbearing one another, and forgiving one another, if any man have a quarrel against any: even as Christ forgave you, so also do ye. And above all these things put on charity, which is the bond of perfectness. And let the peace of God rule in your hearts, to the which also ye are called in one body and be ye thankful. Let the word of Christ, dwell in you richly in all wisdom; teaching and admonishing one another in psalms and hymns and spiritual songs, singing with grace in your hearts to the Lord. And whatsoever ye do in word or deed, do all in the name of the Lord Jesus, giving thanks to God and the Father by him." Colossians chapter 3 v.12 – 17. Study these verses daily. For most single Christians your fight to abstain will be on the forefront of your Christian walk, but you will work on other areas of your Christian walk as you grow. If only we all were seeking God together. Every church would be powerful.

This is a lot for some, but it's necessary. Especially if your pastor doesn't teach this. Don't feel overwhelmed. Just seek the Lord. Take it one day at a time. Fall in love with Jesus. Love the Lord with all of your heart, soul, mind, and spirit. Love praising and worshiping God. Surrender all of your heart unto the Lord. Let the Lord create in you a clean heart and renew the right spirit in you. All of the games from the old man, let them go, yield them to God, and seek the Lord. Let go of those evil deeds and seek the Lord. Let go of sexual crimes and seek the Lord. Let go of all sins and seek the Lord.

Here's another verse on the new man. "That ye put off concerning the former conversation the old man, which is corrupt according to the deceitful lusts; and be renewed in the spirit of your mind; and that ye put on the new man, which after God is created in righteousness and true holiness." Ephesians chapter 4 v. 22 – 24. Once again we hear about lust. Our desire for sex, our sex drive, and our sexual appetites, are they rooted in lust? If it's a spirit of lust, God can remove this from us. If it's our flesh, we need God to give us temperance which is a fruit of the Holy Ghost / Holy Spirit. We need God's help, but we must do our part by yielding ourselves to God. Even Jesus yielded Himself before He was crucified in the garden. Our old conversations that lead to sexual encounters must be yielded to God. Yield all your sex game to God. All of your smooth talk fellas, yield it to God. All of your seductive talk ladies, yield it to God. Put off the old man which is you outside of Christ, and seek the Lord to become the new man in Christ.

"There is therefore now no condemnation to them which are in Christ Jesus, who walk not after the flesh, but after the Spirit." Roman chapter 8 v.1. Because you are after God, the Spirit, God does not condemn you if you commit sin. Why? Because you are seeking Him to be the new man in Christ. You're not walking after the flesh anymore which is the old man. If you are really seeking the Lord and you commit any sin, repent, ask God for forgiveness, and continue to seek God. Don't feel condemned. Although you are guilty because you are seeking God to be the new man in Christ, you have received more grace. Growing in Christ is not an easy task. You must endure your old man as you transition into the new man. You're going to learn many things about yourself in this process. Maybe things you never knew about yourself. I've learned new things about myself. At one time I didn't see everything wrong with me, but as I sought the Lord, one day I saw myself clearly. I wept because I really believed I was a good man. I humbled myself. As you seek the Lord, carry all of your feelings to God in transparent prayers. "Casting all your care upon him; for he careth for you." First Peter chapter 5 v. 7. There will be days that feel like there is no hope of changing. Your old man doesn't want to take a backseat to the new man, but remember, God is the one who will make the changes if you just yield all of you to Him. Romans chapter 6 v. 6 says, "Knowing this, that our old man is crucified with him, that the body of sin might be destroyed, that henceforth we should not serve sin." When we received Jesus our old man was crucified with Jesus. We didn't do anything for our old man to be crucified, we only accepted Jesus. If we seek God and yield, God will make the changes in us to become the new man in Christ. See how easy this is? "Take my yoke upon you, and learn of me; for I am meek and lowly in heart: and ye shall find rest unto your souls. For my yoke is easy, and my burden is light." Matthew chapter 11 v. 29 – 30. Even though it seems hard that's our old man not desiring to change. Just yield yourself with your whole heart unto Christ. Your old man is already crucified with Christ although it doesn't appear that way. Even Apostle Paul had to deal with his old man; his flesh. Romans chapter 7 v. 24. "Humble yourselves therefore under the mighty hand of God, that he may exalt you in due time:" First Peter chapter 5 v. 6. "But he giveth more grace. Wherefore he saith; GOD RESISTETH THE PROUD, BUT GIVETH GRACE UNTO

THE HUMBLE." James chapter 4 v. 6. Humbling yourself is a beautiful thing. God gives you more of His grace when you humble yourself before Him. Humbling yourself to God says to Him that you cannot make it without His intervention. Keep pursuing God if you fall or mess up. This is why we have grace. There is no condemnation. However, for those of you who will not seek God and who will not stop living in sin, you do not receive more grace. Your grace remains at the same measure. You do not receive more grace. You keep the same grace. Only you don't know how much grace this is. You cannot continue in sin and hope grace may abound. Romans chapter 6 v. 1 & 2. Please don't play with your soul.

"Draw nigh to God, and he will draw nigh to you." James chapter 4 v. 8. If we would just seek God's face we will find Him. Seeking God is us drawing close to Him, and in turn He will draw close to us. He will make sure we find Him and learn of Him if we seek Him. I pray these scriptures blessed you. It's time to be real in the Lord.

As we seek the Lord God's gives us His characteristics. We start bearing fruit in His righteousness. We begin to walk in the Spirit. God anoints us to be His ministers of His word. After God anoints us we must continue to fellowship with God. We must continue to do those things we did to receive His anointing. Once you're anointed by God, He will use your gifts to build up His kingdom. This is where some of us get into trouble. If we sin at this level, God still continues to use us with His anointing. This gives a false sense of confidence that you can continue in sin and God is ok with it. "For the gifts and calling of God are without repentance. Romans chapter 11 v. 29. I love the Amplified Bible's version, "For God's gifts and His call are irrevocable. [He never withdraws them when once they are given, and He does not change His mind about those to whom He gives His grace or to whom He sends His call.] Once you're anointed to do something for God, God doesn't take it back. This is why so many people of God get deceived. Somehow sin enters their life and instead of doing those things they once did to receive their anointing, they continue in sin because the anointing is still very present. They really believe it's well. They believe they are truly approved of God although they continue in sin without trying to stop. Once you allow sin to remain in your life without repentance, the old man comes back to life. If you grew up in the church and was never in the world, your situation becomes different. You develop a man that's new to you through your continued sin. You begin to walk in darkness although you're in the church. If you continue in sin without true repentance, evil spirits begin to come into your life and teach you the game you never learned in the world. A different game. A game that uses the word of God and the gifts of God to get what you want out of the daughters of God. Like I said briefly on page 8, the qualities of God can make us look more attractive than those who do not have these qualities. There comes a time when the things of God become attractive qualities. Qualities that women desire in a husband. It may sound crazy to some, but it's true. A woman of God told me this, "Brother Marcus, there are many things I like about you. I don't know what to call it. You can pray. You worship the Lord. You know the bible. It's like I have a spiritual attraction to you. I guess that's what I can call it." The woman of God who said this knew the woman of God I was dating at that time. This caused some confusion, but I understood her point of view. The woman I was dating didn't understand it and was very angry about it. She believed this woman of God was shooting her shot at me, but she wasn't in my opinion. I understood it. When I see a woman of God in passionate worship to God it's beautiful to me. A woman of God walking in revelations of God's word is attractive to me. Don't add some sanctified cuteness to her lol. I believe this is a thing to those of us who become mature in the kingdom of God. Men of God who begin to walk in darkness use these qualities to their advantage. Let's talk about the men of God who are high valued and desired by lots of women of God. He's Boaz in their eyes. Plenty of daughters see him as husband. A son like this shines bright. This sets him apart from other men of God. There are sons who are jealous of this man of God because so many daughters of God want him. Let me go deeper. They are jealous because the woman they specifically sees as wife doesn't see them as husband. Her eyes are on the high valued man of God. She's not considering potential husband material. There are some daughters of God waiting to see if you tap into your potential, but when they see this high valued man of God, the wait is over. You're calling her and she isn't returning your calls anymore. She's not responding to your texts. Potential husband material has been ghosted and when you find out why you're hurt and angry. The high valued brother in Christ has her attention. This is really sad when she's the one you see as wife. This brother has plenty of women's attention while you only want one woman's attention, but he has it. The only issue for these women of God who sees him as husband is how he sees them. Does he see you purely as a sister in the Lord? Does he see you as wife? Or does he see you as a sexual conquest? If he sees you as a sexual conquest, he will play the game according to your level of intelligence. Darkness teaches him which game to play with you. His words will be clever and tailormade just for you. Now ladies if you're not planning on abstaining from sex, which is sin, well, that's on you. If you want to be played, ok, be played. Like I said earlier, once you've given a man your body there's nothing else to give. I've heard so many stories of how certain women of God are in the bedroom. It's so sad. This brother has moved on and you're left heartbroken. He shares your sexual skills. Many men of God would love to be your rebound, and if they succeed, they confirm what they heard about your sex skills. Some women leave the church because they are so embarrassed. I've had reproach before. It spreads to other churches. Best believe other churches know about your sexual abilities and skills. You need to be on high alert. Just like women with reputations, men of God are seeking to get a piece of the action. Stop having sex altogether. Shut it down! Don't date or talk to any man. Seek the Lord and allow God to remove the reproach on your name. Repent and seek the Lord ladies. I'm sorry if this happened to you. I've been there. Church Girl told every detail of our sexual encounters and this information spread to several churches who were connected to us. I made it through and you will too. Don't worry about it. Get to a place where you're not moved by what people are saying about you. I did. I wrote it all in my books. I'm over it. Who cares? I don't anymore. God forgave me and that's all that matters.

Men if you're a son of God, where is your integrity? Do you have any integrity? Do you have an attitude right now reading this? I'm talking to the players in the house of God. I'm not talking to men of God who are really seeking God. I'm talking to the whoremongers preying on the daughters of God. You say you love the Lord and you certainly know how to play church very well, but why are you playing with the hearts of God's daughters? Why sell them a dream? Was it just to have them sexually? Don't start talking about the grace of God right now. "Shall we continue in sin that grace may abound; God forbid." Romans chapter 6 v. 1-2. "God understand I'm a man. There's too many women to choose from and I need to know who's the best choice for me." How? By sleeping with them all? Women of God ask me often, "How come you don't hang out with some of the single brothers in Christ?" Well, many of them aren't trying to abstain. I'm not interested in hearing how any brother slept with a sister in Christ. This got on my last nerve. I would shut them up quickly. I wasn't interested. It grieved me at times. I learned to walk alone. Not all single men in Christ are sexually active, but I grew tired of knowing many were not. When I was at my four year mark of abstinence things hit me very hard. I shared this in book, "From Woman To Woman Volume Two" page 234 paragraph 1.

"My divorce with my first wife was finalized on August 25th, 2005. The day Hurricane Katrina was passing by Miami before it headed to New Orleans. The details of what happened in court and after court are all in my book, "A Pastor's Mistake." After it ended with Sister Friend, I was abstinent four years. During these four years, I learned a lot about the bible, I grew in the Lord, my first book was published in 2007, I was on the dance ministry, and I started a good job April 10, 2006. I let go of the idea of being a nurse. There were several women of God that I tried to date during these years, and I got absolutely nowhere with any of them. The last one I tried to talk to disappeared from our church, and returned pregnant. This pissed me off! I was so pissed I said to God, "Lord, I'm tired of the church! I need a

break from the church!" and I stopped going to church altogether. I wanted to be away from all church folks. "

I'll never forget saying, "Lord, who am I abstaining for? It seems like no one else is abstaining but me." I was in deep anguish to say these words. These words also showed I still needed more growth in Christ. There was more that had me very angry. It was the men of God who also discouraged me. I grew exhausted and I did leave the church for a season, but I didn't lose my belief in Christ. Nowadays I understand my personal walk with Christ is unto the Lord and I can't be moved by the lives of other Christians. I will be accountable for myself and my life before the Lord on judgment day.

I mentioned integrity a little earlier. Joseph is the best example of integrity in the bible. In Genesis chapter 39, Joseph is brought into the home of an Egyptian. The bible says this Egyptian saw the Lord was with Joseph. God blessed his home because of Joseph. Everything Joseph did for the Egyptian prospered. Joseph was greatly favored. The Egyptian's wife tried to have sex with Joseph and Joseph ran away from her. He had a character of integrity. I'm sure she was a very sexy attractive woman. Joseph refused to sleep with her. He refused to be her side piece. He refused to sin against God. Men of God must do better with God's daughters. We must have integrity. Seek the Lord and find your wife. Women of God must have integrity. Seek the Lord and prepare for your husband to find you. As the children of God, we must be honorable to God first and to each other. We must keep God first and respect His word. We must love God and yield our lives to His will. Fall in love with Jesus and allow God to give you real Christian character. Allow God to form you into His word. Don't be phony. Stop being a hypocrite in God's house. As you seek God and go from glory to glory, God will form you into a new man / woman in Christ. God will work on your flaws and cause you to be better in Him. Let God do it. You must seek God with all of your heart, mind, soul, spirit, and strength for this to happen. That's what you did to receive the anointing. Well, that's if you're anointed. You could be in position at a dead religious church that doesn't preach or teach against sin. If this is your reality then this book is a very big eye opener for you. If you're at a church that doesn't teach abstinence your mind is blown away by this book. So I'm pretty sure you're a person who has never searched the bible. If you're this person message me on social media and tell me about your feelings right now in this moment. Be a real Christian. No more games in God's church. Start today. Renounce your sins. Repent. Seek God and move forward. Let your past be your past. Don't worry about reproach or any negative thing said about you. Repent and move forward in Christ.

Study Proverbs chapters 1 – 7. Study Romans chapter 12. If you are in the leadership of the church, First Corinthian chapter 4 v. 2 says stewards, (leadership) should be found faithful. This church was trying to judge Apostle Paul and he set them straight in the love of Christ. In verse 4 Paul says, "he that judgeth me is the Lord." Because Apostle Paul was right in the sight of the Lord this was a huge statement to say to the Corinthian church. In verse 5 Apostle Paul reminds them how God will judge us all when He comes. Where will you stand in your judgement? I pray the Lord says to me, "Well done Marcus. Enter into my rest." I personally believe if we allow Jesus to change us, judgment day will be a happy day for us all. Remember our old man should be hidden in Christ. If your old man is alive and thriving, well, you need to humble yourself and seek the Lord. If you're really seeking God, but you're sincerely struggling, it's going to be ok. Keep seeking the Lord. Micah chapter 7 v.7 – 9 should be one of your power scriptures. I quoted these in tears as I went through my struggles with fornication, watching porn, twerk videos, and lust. "Therefore I will look unto the Lord; I will wait for the God of my salvation: my God will hear me. Rejoice not against me, O mine enemy: when I fall, I shall arise; when I sit in darkness, the Lord shall be a light unto me. I will bear the indignation of the Lord, because I have sinned against him, until he plead my cause, and execute judgment for me: he will bring me forth to the light, and I shall behold his righteousness." Micah chapter 7 v.7 – 9. I received my first anointing when I struggled with lust and masturbation. Here's what I wrote about this experience,

"As I sought the Lord, He began to do some new things inside

of me. One day on my job, I was crying to God because my desire for a woman was burning tremendously and I needed the Lord's intervention. As I cried out to God, I experienced a gentle warmth come upon me. It was such a beautiful feeling and I started saying, "God, is this you?" Since the day this first happened, this warmth was always at my workstation. I have never experienced anything like this before. As I talked to my pastor about it, he let me know that God has given me an anointing. All I knew was that warmth felt very comforting and I welcomed it on my job. Before I was backslidden I spoke in tongues, but I didn't experience anything like this feeling. Moreover, I started seeing what looked like stars appearing and disappearing. I also started seeing dark shadows appear and disappear. I didn't understand what was going on with me, but I shared all of these events with my pastor. Pastor Davis explained, "Your gifts are being birthed and I will train you in your gifts." So, my pastor began explaining the different spiritual gifts I had and gave me the scriptures that backed up what he was saying. I was very appreciative of Pastor Davis. I was so happy God was doing wonderful things in my life, and it made me humble myself even the more." A Pastor's Mistake paragraph 1 page 35.

All though I struggled with my flesh burning, God anointed me. Why? It's not about being perfect to receive God's anointing. It's about your heart being pure toward Him. King

David slept with Uriah's wife, got her pregnant, had Uriah killed, and married her. Second Samuel chapter 11. The very last verse says, "The thing that David had done displeased the Lord." King David reaped what he sowed in sin. However, when Prophet Samuel was giving King Saul the word of the Lord, God said David was a man after God's own heart. First Samuel chapter 13 v. 14. The man after God's own heart committed adultery and murder. If your heart is in the right place, God may give you more grace when He should be judging you severely. King Saul sinned and was judged severely, and lost his reign as king. King David sinned and was judged, but did not lose his reign as king. I know most of you reading this book will say, "I know I have a good heart." Here's what the word of God says, "The heart is deceitful above all things, and desperately wicked; who can know it?" Jeremiah chapter 17 v. 9. Look at verse 10, "I the Lord search the heart, I try the reins, even to give every man according to his ways, and according to the fruit of his doings." Let's look at Galatians chapter 6 v. 7, "Be not deceived; God is not mocked: for whatsoever a man soweth, that shall he also reap." Even if we sin with a pure heart there are consequences to our doings. Just think players, all of those women you used, hurt, and threw away like they were nothing, you're going to reap what you sowed. You just don't know how you're going to reap it. Even if you repent right now and turn your heart to God right now, you're still going to reap what you did to all of those women. Do you have a daughter? Would you want a man to treat your daughter like you're treating God's daughters? What if you finally find the woman you truly see as wife and you reap what you did to other women through her? She uses you, destroys your heart, and throws you away as if you're nothing. Then she gossips about it and brags how she dogged you out. When you reap it just know it's going to hurt you in ways you really couldn't imagine. Maybe it will be a combination of pain you couldn't even comprehend. Please repent and turned to God. The sooner the better. I've reaped things. Before I could open my mouth to complain vocally, a flashback of when I did that same thing went through my mind. When you reap it you're going to know. God will make sure you know. The best thing you can do in this moment is not add anything else to be reaped in your future. Humble yourself. Seek the Lord and may God give you His grace as you reap everything you sowed by hurting God's daughters. Same thing goes for you daughters who have used the men of God. You took his money and knew you weren't interested in him. You played the game to get your bills paid or get the things you couldn't afford on your own. You made him believe you were into him, but you weren't. You're going to reap it.

To those of you who have been hurt by someone and you desire God to get them. You want them to reap what they sowed. You can't wait to hear what happened to them because they hurt you. "Rejoice not when thine enemy falleth, and let not thine heart be glad when he stumbleth: Lest the Lord see it, and it displease him, and he turn away his wrath from him." Proverbs chapter 24 v. 17. How do you feel right now? Ask God to purify your heart. Ask God to help you forgive them. If you want God to get them, God will delay their reaping season.

There are women of God who I fornicated with and I honestly believe sin destroyed our future together. In hind sight I know I missed out. I'm left with memories of our sexual escapades I will never have again with her. You men of God who are bragging, what do you get out of this? You're so happy you had her sexually. As for me I despise many of my sexual memories. I would rather have the woman continuously instead of a sinful memory. What if we messed up the plan of God by sinning? I'm considering writing a book about the good women I missed out on. It's a painful reality when you get an epiphany about a woman you no longer have access to who would have been perfect for your life. I'll come back to this.

Men if you already know this woman exists and you still have access to her, why aren't you putting a ring on her finger? Do you want to get all of your whoring out first and then marry her? She might get married to the next man of God. Stop playing games. If you lose this type of woman you will regret it. Maybe for the rest of your life. I had to pray and ask God to help me let her go. She is gone from my life, but I was still holding on.

She's married to a good man now who loves her and treats her like a queen. Seeing her happy without me was very painful. Think of this you whoremongers. She's gone forever. You didn't think any other man would come along for her. God is faithful. Get it together, seek the Lord, pursue her, and marry her while you have the chance. Women of God this goes for you too. You know this man loves you, adores you, but he's just an option because you believe you deserve better. Better how? Keep it up and one day that same man will let you go. He will choose another woman who will immediately embrace him. You will watch him get married and you could regret it for the rest of your life. Seeing the person you could have been with happy and enjoying life with the next person hurts. Stop acting like it doesn't hurt. It hurt me. I cried. Oh how I cried when I saw my error. "Time and chance happeneth to us all." Ecclesiastes chapter 9 v. 11. God will send at least one person in our lifetime that would make us a great spouse and we would be a great spouse for them. It's up to us to recognize what God is doing. If you're not seeking God and you're playing games, you can miss this person. You must remember that every one of us has a "will" of our own. God is not going to force us to marry anyone. You want to marry her, but she doesn't want to marry you. You want to marry him, but he has his eye on another woman. Sometimes we just don't like who God sent our way. Just say it. I know a woman of God who's been waiting more than twenty years for her husband. I asked, "Are you sure you didn't miss your husband?" She paused and thought as I watched her think. God is faithful people. She didn't want or like who God sent her way. Our two "wills" must be in agreement to get married. You add this to all the other issues we have as Christian singles and you see why marriage is taking forever. If we all would seek the Lord and allow our new man to be formed in Christ we would see so many more marriages.

I don't believe in God telling us to marry a specific person. I know God did this with the Prophet Hosea, but let's be real. God told Hosea to marry a whore with children of whoredom. Hosea chapter 1 v. 2. Was this being equally yoked? Of course not. A prophet of God marrying a whore is not normal. The whore's name is Gomer. Gomer didn't even know who the fathers were for her children. No DNA testing back then. What man was going to claim the children of a whore? Especially in those days. Show me anyone else in the bible who got married because God told them to do it? Not even Adam. Adam woke up and said, "This is now bone of my bone, and flesh of my flesh." He knew without God telling him. You also don't see anyone in the bible getting married because of prophecy. That's how I got married to my first wife. How many people do you see in the bible getting married because of a dream? Or getting married by someone saying to a person, "God says you're my husband / wife." I have a complete teaching on all of these in my book, "Tainted

Influence. Identifying Prophetic Truth & Error" in Chapter Six "Married By Prophecy & Dreams." Page 181 – 183.

God is not the author of confusion. You ever noticed how much confusion follows people who say they had a dream that they married you? Or maybe they heard a voice say that you are their wife or husband. There is always some type of confusion surrounding anyone who received prophecy to get married. I tell my friends, and anyone who asks me, if anyone says that God said you are supposed to marry them run for your life. This is manipulation folks. God does not go against our will and He is not going to make you do anything. Marriage is honorable in all according to Hebrews chapter 13 verse 4, but if it's against your will how honorable is it?

Saints of God please do not marry anyone against your will. Do not allow a dream, prophecy, or anything else make you marry someone you don't have any interest in. It's one thing if you two were engaged and prophecy comes to confirm your union, but don't let prophecy or dreams be the reason you are married. When you marry someone because of prophecy you're only doing it because your desire is to be in the perfect will of God, but you are not in love with them. Where is the love? You're going to marry someone and hope love comes into the picture later. I remember when I was getting married because of prophecy, it seemed like we were embarking on having heaven in our marriage, but it was just the opposite. If one of the two people do not want the other and has no interest in the person they are prophesied to marry, this is going to cause a great dilemma, but again, there is no passionate love in the foundation. It's a disaster in the making if they get married. I want to quote Apostle Ivory Hopkins from his book "Angel Of Light In Marriage." He says on page 11 paragraph 1, "When God puts people together, there will be a mutual pursuit, not one fatally attracted to the other." This is very powerful and sobering. Single people please purchase this book because it will help you. ORDER IT NOW! (www.pilgrimsministry.com) Prophecy and counsel should never violate your free will. When you don't desire someone, you just don't desire them. It's not a sin because you're not interested in the person. I was completely miserable being married to a woman because of prophecy. My gifts and love tokens were all garbage to her and it was impossible for me to please her in any way. Do you really want to live what I went through?

I hate to say it so directly ladies of God. There are times in the Lord when it appears some women of God have almost lost their minds when it pertains to being married. In a former church there were three different women of God who approached me saying, "God says you're my husband." Well, somebody was lying and it was all three of them. If you say these words to me, I'm running for my life. If you say you had a dream about us getting married, I'm not moved by it. If you tell me you had a dream that we had sex, I'm not moved by it. People of God we better watch as well as pray and seek the Lord. We are so deceived by all of these church games. Men, and women of God, if you're going to shoot your shot, please do it decently and in order. Be respectful. Be honorable. Most of all keep the Lord at the center of your courtship / dating experience. Do not use dreams, visions, or voices to get someone to marry you. Do not want someone so bad that you will do practically anything to make them yours. Please do not resort to manipulative games to get someone to marry you. Do not use the old man to try to get married. Use the new man to get married through Christ.

While you're seeking God to make yourself better, yield your desire to be married to God. We all have things we desire in our future spouse. The reason why I suggested you yield your marriage desire to God is because your desire is going to be enhanced by God. As you grow from glory to glory your desires are going to change. I used to have a long list for a wife and this list contained how she should physically look. As I grew in the Lord it expanded to add Christian qualities. After my recent marriage failed, I received professional counseling for a year. My therapist / counselor asked me to write a list of the things I desire in a wife. I did my homework. After I completed my assignment, the Holy Ghost spoke to me hours later. "Marcus, are you sure you've completed your list? Read it over." I read my list and I said, "Yes. I'm finished." The Holy Ghost responded, "Did you realize that you didn't write any physical qualities you desire in her body?" Honestly, I didn't know and neither did I add any physical qualities to the list. My desires have changed. What I desired thirty years ago is not what I desire now. What is it that you need in a spouse? What are the things you want in a spouse? If you meet this person, will God be at the center of it? Will you two seek God together as a couple? Men can you lead her in the things of God like prayer and praise and worship? Men will you love her like Christ loves the church? Women will you respect him? I hope these are some good thoughts for you. Let's talk about the new man a little more.

Like I said previously, yield yourself unto God. Let's say it in a better way, yield your old man to the Lord, and allow the Lord to make you into a new man in Christ. Here's a power scripture. Meaning you need to study this verse until it's in your subconscious. Romans chapter 13 v. 14, "But put ye on the Lord Jesus Christ, and make not provision for the flesh, to fulfill the lusts thereof." While you're dating / courting make no plans to have sexual sin. Think of everything you do prior to having sex. Did you just think of those things? Good. Now don't do any of them anymore. You're accountable. You're accountable for prepping to have sex. How ever you hook up, meet up, or connect, do not do those things anymore. Cologne, perfume, lingerie, grey sweats, heels, haircuts, etc. All of your preparation routines prior to having sex, yield them to God in prayer. Put on the Lord Jesus Christ. Put on prayer, studying the word of God, praise, worship, intercession, and fasting. Do not make any more provisions to have sex. Don't buy anything new for having sex. Amen? Amen.

Galatians chapter 5 v. 19, "Now the works of the flesh are manifest, which are these; adultery, fornication, uncleanness, lasciviousness, idolatry, witchcraft, hatred, variance, emulations, wrath, strife, seditions, heresies, envyings, murders, drunkenness, revellings, and such like: of the which I tell you before, as I have also told you in times past, that they which do such things shall not inherit the kingdom of God." If we are doing these things, we shall not inherit the kingdom of God. Yield the old man to Christ and seek the face of the Lord.

Ephesians chapter 4 v. 22 – 24, "That ye put off concerning the former conversation the old man, which is corrupt according to the deceitful lusts; and be renewed in the spirit of your mind; And that ye put on the new man, which after God is created in righteousness and true holiness." Read the rest of this chapter. It's time to seek the face of God so we can all be changed into the new man which is after God.

Philippians chapter 1 v. 27, "Only let your conversation be as it becometh the gospel of Christ: that whether I come and see you, or else be absent, I may hear of your affairs, that ye stand fast in one spirit, with one mind striving together for the faith of the gospel;" Our conversations need to become the gospel. We shouldn't be adding fuel to our hot burning flesh by asking, "What do you like sexually?" If you are truly getting married, I recommend a mature sexual conversation prior to marriage. What do I mean by truly getting married? You're officially engaged. What's officially engaged? The ring is on her finger with a wedding date and wedding venue scheduled on the calendar. No it's not ok to have sex because you are getting married. If you can't wait until your wedding day then get married immediately. Go to the courthouse or have a small private wedding with those closest to the both of you, and have your major wedding event later. Don't get it twisted. Are we of the body of Christ or not?

Most of us are or were sexually active. We are in three different categories: never married, divorced, and widowed. We all come from different backgrounds. If you're reading this book then you're probably a Christian. Why are you a Christian? Did you really give your life to Jesus? Or is your life still your own? Meaning you're doing everything you want and Jesus Christ doesn't appear anywhere in your life. Is your old man still thriving? Please put in the work so God can help you become a new man in Christ. Regardless of what you were taught in your church or heard through society, God's word is right. If your church isn't teaching all of the word of God, God's word is still right. Here's a verse that should be a power verse in your life, "Work out your own salvation with fear and trembling."

Philippians chapter 2 v. 12. Please don't only listen to your pastor. You have to put in the personal work to become the new man in Christ Jesus. "Examine yourselves, whether ye be in the faith; prove your own selves. Know ye not your own selves, how that Jesus Christ is in you, except ye be reprobates?" Second Corinthians chapter 13 v. 5.

Reprobate: a morally unprincipled person.

One who is predestined to damnation.

Shameless.

If you do not know the word of God, how can you examine yourself? In order to become a new creature in Christ Jesus you must seek the face of God. You must spend time in God's presence. You must learn the bible and you must pray. Not just prayer requests, but prayers asking God to cleanse your life. Prayers to become more like Jesus. Prayers to walk in righteousness and holiness. Let's continue.

Within those three categories are those who were molested and/or raped, and lgbtq. Bring your old man and your traumas to God. I have an ex who was molested, raped, and gang raped. Some of us have experienced some very evil and brutal things. Bring it to God. I now understand that everyone who was molested as a child didn't find those experiences traumatic. I was very shocked when a man, and two women, shared their experience with me. How the molestation was presented and executed, the three of them enjoyed the sex. I couldn't believe my ears. There are people who were molested, but they enjoyed it. They looked forward to it. They were excited about it. This opened my eyes. I searched the internet and found others like them. There are plenty of rape victims who had orgasms during the rape although they did not consent. Their body responded to sexual stimulation. If you were raped please get some help and talk about it. Do not carry anymore guilt because your body orgasmed during the rape. Please get some professional help. I never considered anyone having a soul tie with someone who raped or molested them. Yield all of your sexual experiences to God. Whether you liked it or hated it, consented or not consented, please yield them all to God. Let the Lord purge you from your past and make you whole. Get some help please.

I've mentioned and talked about the Holy Spirit / Holy Ghost. Here's a question. "Have ye received the Holy Ghost since ye believed?" Acts chapter 19 v. 2. If you have not received the Holy Spirit, you need to ask God to fill you. If you've been taught the Holy Ghost isn't real, you were taught wrong. Once again, are you a partial son or daughter? "So then they that are in the flesh cannot please God. But ye are not in the flesh, but in the Spirit, if so be that the Spirit of God dwell in you. Now if any man have not the Spirit of Christ, he is none of his." Romans chapter 8 v. 8 & 9. If you do not have the Holy Spirit, well, do you belong to Christ? Let's see how the Amplified Bible translates this verse. "So then those who are living the life of the flesh [catering to the appetites and impulses of their carnal nature] cannot please or satisfy God, or be acceptable to Him. But you are not living the life of the flesh, you are living the life of the Spirit, if the [Holy] Spirit of God [really] dwells within you [directs and controls you]. But if anyone does not possess the [Holy] Spirit of Christ, he is none of His [he does not belong to Christ, is not truly a child of God]." If you do not believe in the Holy Ghost, or if you deny the existence of the Holy Ghost, then you cannot receive the Holy Ghost. Receiving the Holy Spirit is foundational in our salvation. Here's the foundational bible verse, "Then Peter said unto them, Repent, and be baptized every one of you in the name of Jesus Christ for the remission of sins, and ye shall receive the gift of the Holy Ghost. For the promise is unto you, and to your children and to all that are afar off, even as many as the Lord our God shall call." Act chapter 2 v. 38 & 39. This is the word of God and it's a promise to you and your children. It's a gift. It's your gift if you received Jesus. Are you rejecting this gift? How can you be a Christian and not believe this? If your pastor doesn't believe this and teaches against this, why are they still your pastor? Unless you're in a cult that has you isolated somewhere, pray about resigning from that church and moving on to more in Christ. Everything you do not believe in the word of God limits your experience in Christ. Unbelief is an enemy. Jesus was limited in doing miracles because of their unbelief. Mark chapter 6 v. 5 & 6. Everything your pastor teaches you with unbelief hinders your walk with Christ. Ask God to purify your heart and mind of every seed of unbelief you were taught in the bible. Maybe it's your mom or dad, or someone else teaching you unbelief. Ask God to wash you of all unbelief. Don't be a partial Christian. We all need the Holy Spirit / Holy Ghost. This is the major difference maker. Roman 8 v. 1, "There is therefore now no condemnation to them which are in Christ Jesus, who walk not after the flesh, but after the Spirit." When you're seeking God's face and in pursuit of growth in Christ, you are walking in the Spirit if you are filled with the Holy Ghost. You are not condemned because of the sin in your life if you're seeking God and walking in the Spirit. If you're not seeking God you cannot grow in grace. The mature Christians should know this information. I'm writing this for those of you who are in churches that don't teach everything. Here's what I said in "Tainted Influence" paragraph 1, page 128 on unbelief.

If you say you are a believer of the bible, you are saying that you believe the entire bible. You cannot believe certain parts of the bible and reject other sections of the bible. God's thoughts are not our thoughts and His ways are not our ways; you can read it for yourself in Isaiah chapter 55. God is who He is and whatever He does is right even if we don't understand His way of doing things. This is how many people of God end up in error although they started their walk with God correctly. You cannot

Marcus L. Boston

build a doctrine off of a few scriptures. How can you only believe certain sections of the bible and negate other sections of the bible, but call yourself a Holy Spirit Christian believer? I can boldly say that you do not have the Holy Spirit and that you are a deceiver not a believer. This is why we have so many denominations today throughout the world, and why we have so many man-made, fleshly, and demonic doctrines. Furthermore, I would like to add that it's amazing that we all have the same book, but do not see eye to eye about its contents. This is why we all need to be filled with the Holy Spirit / Holy Ghost so God can teach us exactly what He means in His word. Without being taught by God we can all be in error concerning the bibles pure meaning. Even the people of God who sincerely live for God can eventually walk in doctrinal error if we are not careful.

Please believe the word of God. Don't limit what God can do for you in your life. It's extremely important that you seek the Lord personally. You cannot just believe your pastor and not seek the Lord on your own. There's more in God for you outside of what your pastor is teaching. Seeking God allows Him to make the changes within you that He desires. It gives you more grace for the struggles with the flesh. You become better and do better through Christ. It won't make you perfect, but you'll be better. You'll learn and gain strength to stand on the word of God. I pray you're convicted and desire to seek the Lord. You cannot become a new man in Christ without seeking Christ and you cannot become a new man without being filled with the Holy Spirit. You need both. Will you pay the price? Will you put in the tearful work?

People of God seek the Lord. Forget about the sex games. You have to start seeing sex how God sees it. God created sex for married couples. All sex outside of marriage is sin. Men of God, please stop using God's daughters and daughters of God, stop giving up your body before marriage. Remember we reap what we sow. Bring all of your sexual desires to God in prayer as you seek the Lord. If you're a real virgin, maybe I should change how I'm saying this? If you're a pure virgin, please stay a pure virgin. Be that pure gift on your wedding night. Your future spouse should be humbled and amazed they married someone who has never received or given anyone an orgasm. Their entire body is unexplored from head to toe. No soul ties. No one to compare. Enjoy sex to the fullest when you're married. Do not show anyone your naked body. You've waited this long. You might as well keep waiting. Do not allow anyone to do anything to you that could cause you to have an orgasm and do not do anything to anyone that could make them orgasm. It's all sin singles. All of these acts defile our bodies unless you're married. By the way, oral sex is found in the book of, "Song of Solomon." That's for the preachers who believe oral sex is an abomination. Have fun finding it. For all non-pure virgins like the one I shared in this book, please stop those other sexual activities. Ask God to help you. Singles may God help us all. Some singles who read this book have rejected this information. That's ok with me. I wrote what God told me to write. Did you really receive Jesus? Some of you don't want to know the bible because you believe if you don't know what's in the bible you won't be held accountable. Luke chapter 12 v. 48, "But he that knew not, and did commit things worthy of stripes, shall be beaten with few stripes." I would rather not be beaten at all. Amen. You're still accountable in your ignorance. As a matter of fact, "And the times of this ignorance God winked at; but now commandeth all men every where to repent:" Act chapter 17 v. 30. Lgbtq bring it to God and seek the Lord. God didn't form you to be that way.

Singles let's all abstain until we get married. Well, if we get married. A man and a woman "wills" must line up and with all of our issues, ..., well, ... may God help us. One thing is certain: we will all be judged one day. "For we must all appear before the judgment seat of Christ; that every one may receive the things done in his body, according to that he hath done, whether it be good or bad." Second Corinthians chapter 5 v. 10. Everything we do with our bodies is going to be judged. Yeah I know, some of y'all never heard your pastor preach this. For the pastors who are teaching on abstinence, continue in excellence.

I had no intention to write this book. This book was an assignment and I pray it ministered to you. Let's all seek the Lord while He may be found. None of us know the day or the hour we will leave this earth. Let's be ready. God bless you.

Verses to study.

"It is good for a man not to touch a woman. Nevertheless, to avoid fornication, let every man have his own wife, and let every woman have her own husband."

First Corinthians chapter 7 v. 1 & 2.

"Flee also youthful lusts: but follow righteousness, faith, charity (love), peace, with them that call on the Lord out of a pure heart."

Second Timothy chapter 2 v. 22

"I will lift up mine eyes unto the hills, from whence cometh my help. My help cometh from the Lord, which made heaven and earth."

Psalm 121 v. 1 & 2

Jesus said, "Search the scriptures; for in them ye think ye have eternal life: and they are they which testify of me."

John chapter 5 v. 39

Marcus L. Boston

Jesus said, "But the hour cometh, and now is, when the true worshipers shall worship the Father in spirit and in truth: for the Father seeketh such to worship him. God is a Spirit: and they that worship him must worship him in spirit and in truth."

John chapter 4 v. 23 & 24

Jesus said, "If ye love me, keep my commandments. And I will pray the Father, and he shall give you another Comforter, that he may abide with you for ever, Even the Spirit of truth; whom the world cannot receive, because it seeth him not, neither knoweth him: but ye know him; for he dwelleth with you, and shall be in you. I will not leave you comfortless: I will come to you."

John chapter 14 v. 15 – 18 (Verses on the Holy Ghost / Holy Spirit before the book of Acts. This promise and gift is yours. Be encouraged if were taught wrong. Build up your belief. Ask God to remove doubt and unbelief, and receive your gift.)

"For godly sorrow worketh repentance."

Second Corinthians chapter 7 v. 10

"the goodness of God leadeth thee to repentance?"

Romans chapter 2 v. 4

About The Author

Marcus L. Boston is the owner of Unfazed Publishing LLC. He's been a published author since 2007 and shares his entire life in transparency to minister to others. He is a Christian of thirty years and has written many books to aid Christians in their walks with Christ. His first book, "A Pastor's Mistake. What To Do When You Know Your Pastor Is Wrong," sparked a lot of controversy and criticism. Marcus was attacked by various Christians thinking he was using real names and exposing people with personal attacks. After these Christians discovered that all names were changed and that the book was written respectfully, he began to get some better reviews.

His trademark in writing is being very transparent. He shares his life in truth in an effort to show non-Christians the grace that God has for himself, is the same grace God has for them. He shares his failures in an effort to help others avoid the same pitfalls he experienced; especially those who didn't grow up in the church. His personal theme is,

"Making The Church A Better Place"

Marcus L. Boston

Book Me

Would you like to book me for an appearance or speaking engagement? Would you like autographed books? Would you like to become an author with me? Contact me.

info@marcuslboston.world

www.MarcusLBoston.world

224.762.2242

UNFAZED PUBLISHING
YOUR MIND IS OUR BUSINESS

Become an author with me.

Set up a free writing consultation today.

www.unfazedpublishing.com

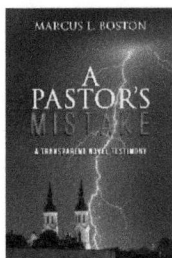

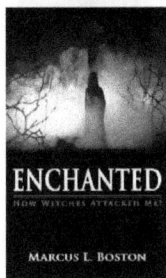

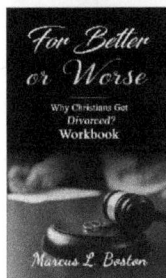

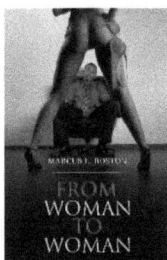

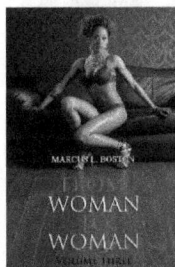

Extremely Transparent. Reader Discretion is Advised. Age 18 +

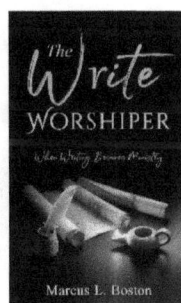

Available On Amazon - Kindle - IBooks

Marcus L. Boston

www.ingramcontent.com/pod-product-compliance
Lightning Source LLC
Chambersburg PA
CBHW050350280326
41933CB00010BA/1404